The Iron-Bound Coast

The Iron-Bound Coast

Karekare in the Early Years

Wallace Badham

Edited by Bob Harvey

PUBLISHER'S NOTE
Wallace Badham's diaries have been reproduced with the minimum of copy-editing, so as to retain his voice. A structural edit has altered the sequence of sections in order to follow chronological order. Dates, personal names and place names have been corrected.

Published by Libro International, an imprint of Oratia Media Ltd,
783 West Coast Road, Oratia, Auckland 0604, New Zealand
www.oratiamedia.com

Copyright © Wallace Badham
Copyright in images © Badham Family Archives and Bob Harvey
  unless specified on p.200
Copyright in this edition © Oratia Media 2009

The copyright holders assert their moral rights in the work.

This book is copyright. Except for the purposes of fair reviewing, no part of this publication may be reproduced or transmitted in any form or by any means, whether electronic, digital or mechanical, including photocopying, recording, any digital or computerised format, or any information storage and retrieval system, including by any means via the Internet, without permission in writing from the publisher. Infringers of copyright render themselves liable to prosecution.

ISBN 978-1-877514-01-2

First published 2009

Editor: Carolyn Lagahetau
Designer: Dee Murch
Proofreader: Anna Fomison

Typeset in Palatino 10/13.5 pt; display and column font Gauntlet
Printed in China by Nordica

Front cover: (foreground) Locals crowd around Captain J.D. Hewett's Gipsy Moth, Karekare Beach, January 1932; (background) The view from the South Point looking back towards The Watchman. Courtesy the Badham family.
Back cover: *Farleys Creek, Karekare*, Essie Johnson, 1911. Courtesy Bob Harvey; photographed by Chris Hoult (www.chphotography.co.nz)
Endpapers: (front) Looking south from the Fishing Rocks; (back) Wallace Badham atop the Big Cone in 1928. Courtesy the Badham family.

Contents

Acknowledgements	6		
Note on weights and measures	8		
Introduction — Bob Harvey	9		
Dedication — Wally Badham	16		
My forebears	17	1931	141
Karekare characters and recollections	37	1932	151
Timber milling on the West Coast	49	1933	159
1914	71	1934	165
1919	73	1935	173
1920	77	1936	177
1923	89	1937	181
1924	95	1938	185
1925	99	1939	189
1926	115	1942	191
1927	121		
1928	125	Epilogue — Lisa Fallow	195
1930	133	Photo acknowledgements	200

Acknowledgements
Bob Harvey

Wally Badham wrote his memoirs of his Karekare years as a personal gift to his niece, Raewyn, and they were subsequently transcribed by Lisa Fallow. I felt that they needed to be seen by a wider audience. Sadly, Wally died before a group of us, who had read the manuscript, could make it possible.

I would like to offer thanks to the following people, who have helped make *The Iron-Bound Coast* possible.

Lisa Fallow has always been enthusiastic about the manuscript, generously helping me with my other books on the West Coast.

John 'Bunny' Badham, son of John, Wally's brother, has assisted greatly, sharing his extensive knowledge of the family, and his photographic collection.

Julie King, daughter of Eileen, Wally's sister, has been enthusiastic in her research, sharing her photographic collections and albums, and providing contacts with her mother Eileen's many friends.

Lisa, John and Julie have been our greatest friends and the proofreaders of this publication: checking details, captions and photographic authenticity.

A special thank you must go to Warwick Badham, Wally's son, who kindly shared his memories of his mother and father with me.

Appreciation is due to Keith Fulljames of Titirangi for allowing us to view and use photographs from his collection and to share his stories of the Karekare boarding-house days.

I would like to thank Waitakere City Council Libraries for permission to reprint from the extensive and magnificent photographic collections, and in particular Robyn Mason, collections advisor, for arranging technical reproduction and sharing her knowledge of the collections.

Thanks to Auckland City Libraries, the Alexander Turnbull Library and the Auckland War Memorial Museum for their kind permission to include photographs held in their collections.

It is with gratitude that I thank a small group of businesses and organisations in Waitakere City who have financially supported this project and whose love of the history of the West has made this publication possible:

Peter Dowling of Oratia Media; friend, mentor and publisher, thank you for seeing the potential in Wally's manuscript.

Murray Spearman and his team at the Portage Waitakere Trusts generously started our funding off. Brent Gore of Titirangi's famed Hardware Café and Kim Mackie, Arts Patron and CEO of Cambridge Clothing, New Lynn added their support. Mark Ford of Watercare Services continued the backing of Waitakere history and publishing he has provided over the last decade, and Mark Gunton of New Zealand Retail Property Group, who is creating history with his investment and vision for Waitakere's future, also provided valuable support.

Acknowledgement is also due to the Creative Communities New Zealand Scheme for their assistance to Oratia Media for completion of the project.

A publishing team of talented locals has brought the book to fruition. Vanessa Sherer did the early work in typing and interpreting Wally's script with acuity. Carolyn Lagahetau added her skill and expertise in working with the original manuscript; our gratitude for her sharp eye for detail and rhythm of language. Dee Murch created the design and brought together all the elements into the final, polished package. Anna Fomison gave an insightful proofread.

In this, the twentieth year of the City of Waitakere, we can add another piece to the jigsaw of our past.

Note on weights and measures

Imperial measures have been retained from the original manuscript. Conversions are as follows:

Length
1 inch = 2.54 centimetres
1 foot = 12 inches = 30.48 centimetres
3 feet = 1 yard = 91.44 centimetres
1 super foot = 0.00236 cubic metres

Area
1 acre = 0.405 hectare

Volume
1 gallon = 4.546 litres

Weight
1 pound = 0.4536 kilogram
1 ton = 1.016 tonnes

Money
12 pence = 1 shilling
20 shillings = 1 pound = $2 (value at decimal conversion in 1967)

Introduction
Bob Harvey

During the final months of his life, I collected Wally Badham from a rest-home in Pakuranga, a seaside suburb of Manukau City, where he had lived for a number of years. I tucked him up in blankets and a couple of pillows and took him for a nostalgic and final trip to the West Coast, back to his beloved Karekare. He was frail and quite weak but, as we got to the Oratia foothills, his spirits lifted and he started to talk about the old road that was once the only road to the West Coast.

Above us the misty Waitakere Ranges stretched from Titirangi in the south, to Taupaki in the distant north, book-ended by the defining mountain peaks of Titirangi and Waiatarua (translated as 'the sound of two oceans'). We could see the Waitemata Harbour and gulf and hear the Tasman Sea to the west and, on the skyline to the north near the end of the Ranges, the great lookout Pukematekeo.

With the sound of two oceans in their ears, guests would travel to Winchelsea House from the Waikumete Rail Station along the muddy unsealed West Coast Road by wagon and coach. The Waikumete area was later renamed Glen Eden, and for 60 years this was the pick-up point for guests arriving who needed transport to the Coast. In his memoirs Wally talks of waiting for the train to arrive in the cold Glen Eden morning. He would have risen early, milked the cows in the dark and then headed off with his uncle or father to pick up the guests and bring them proudly back over the Ranges to Winchelsea House, their holiday destination.

This was the place of Wally's boyhood and our visit gave rise to a flood of memories for him that day. He became very lucid, remembering every bend and where settlers' shanties were but have long since gone now, engulfed by the bush. We paused at the Waiatarua lookout where, in Wally's day, horses were rested and cars were steamed and prepared for the final leg of the journey. From here travellers would fear the worst as they were about to face a two- to three-hour hell trip down Piha Road, which in winter was no more than a mud track and in summer would throw up bone-shaking ruts. The trip always held a modicum of uncertainty as to whether the visitors would reach Winchelsea House by nightfall or not.

I first met Wally while researching material for my book, *The Untamed Coast*. Some of his relatives warned me off making contact with him, telling me he was a recluse, often distant and grumpy. At that time, he lived in a small flat in Howick. When I called to see him and told him I was writing about old Karekare, we struck up an instant rapport. I found a man full of wonderful memories, rich in stories and humour, but I also found someone who had never really gotten over his youth at Karekare.

In the months that followed we became close. I interviewed him extensively. His memory was extraordinary. He seemed to know every part of Karekare, every gully, stream and bush track. I returned many times to talk about his flying years and the family and the guest house, which had been the centre of his life for so many years. I also realised that Wally had lived through some of the most exciting years of the twentieth century including the development of the motor car and solo-piloted aircraft, both of which fascinated him. Throughout the war years and the Great Depression, he had observed the social history of New Zealand and, for over 60 years, the richness of life, people and their stories, much of which had come to him via the hundreds of guests at Karekare. What a place it was and is, this wild, beautiful black sand beach on Auckland's West Coast.

His grandparents purchased the farm and homestead, the northern side of Karekare Valley, from Charles Murdoch Primrose in 1900 and added to it in 1902 with the purchase of the southern side from Abel Lovett. The lush green valley had been originally settled by the Shaw brothers, John and Silas, in 1870, who had come south to Auckland to escape Hone Heke's burning of Kororareka (Russell). The brothers built two houses, one each, at opposite ends of the valley. They were massive men — giants of the bush who could carry anvils on their shoulders, pioneer settlers, millers and road builders. They had run sheep and hacked and cut the treacherous and impossibly steep road down from the valley. The road was known as the Cutting and still bears that name and was used as access to the Henderson and faraway Auckland markets. Around Windy Point South, at low tide the long beach became a much travelled highway to the Whatipu wharf, where many guests would arrive from the port at Onehunga, rather than travelling the uncertain West Coast and Piha roads.

During the late nineteenth century the West Coast, with its rugged cliffs and surf, was a magnet for photographers and painters. Frank and Walter Wright, Charles Blomfield and Alfred Sharpe all painted the roaring seascapes. The Burton brothers journeyed west, laden with large-format cameras and tripods, and photographed the headlands and the bays of the Manukau Harbour, as had Radcliffe, Godber and Winkelmann, photographing for lavish publications and large format framed prints.

Much of Karekare's buildings and farms are the legacy of the Murdoch family. Murdoch was the mill manager of the Karekau Mill situated at the junction of the Opal Pool and Karekare Stream. It was Murdoch, a father of nine, who built the grand guest-house in 1881. The farm and homestead was sold to Wally's grandfather, Charles Farley, in 1900. Murdoch, an ingenious engineer as well as an astute miller, had piped water from the main waterfall along a jarrah trough of five-metre lengths of timber to get the water to a flume. The water dropped downwards from the flume and in turn drove a pelten wheel to operate the flax mill below (the timber mill became a flax mill after timber resources had been exhausted). The flume generated power for the house. The water race was an obsession of Wally's and it figures prominently in his story, as does the amazing bush tram system that traversed the valley and beach landscape, all the way from Skids Gully at the end of the valley to the south rocks and down to Whatipu. At the time, this was one of the most amazing engineering structures in New Zealand. Even today, the complexities of operating it are overwhelming; something also well-covered by Wally in his memoirs. The bush mill systems and the kauri dams' network are part of Waitakere history and their remains can be seen today, silent reminders of a massive industry.

In the latter part of the nineteenth and early part of the twentieth centuries, demand for timber was on the rise. Bullock teams, bush traction engines and tramways were the modes of transportation from dam to mill and then on to cutters and scows. Between 1850 and 1927 there were 72 dams in the Waitakere area alone. Sometimes massive dams built at the head of deep valleys were held back by lakes of felled kauri logs, which could be tripped by simply pulling a single wire. The watery rush as the water and kauri logs poured out and down the ravines could be heard as far away as Auckland City like a rumble as loud as distant thunder.

The Karekare Incline, as it was known, was connected by rail and hauler houses, with its counterpart on the other side of the vast Piha sawmill. Both Piha and Karekare were working mill valleys. Each day the bush trams and trolleys would work logs and sawn timber along the coastline. The Karekare section was the most complex. To haul a log from the Piha Mill to the top of the incline would take two full trolleys coming down the Karekare side. Each weekday six full loads passed over the hill tramway, then three on Saturdays, but no work on Sundays. The wagons on the line comprised of 11 double-bogie trolleys, each with a capacity of 3000 super-feet of timber. These would all travel past the Karekare guest-house.

On the beach the little Sandfly engine worked the rail line down the coast, precariously hugging the cliffs. The line, on sand and trestles, was continually swept by massive surf, which would constantly destroy sections of it. Today, the rail tracks have long been taken up and the bush has reclaimed any vestiges of this massive network. Along the sand-flats of the coast from the south Karekare rocks to the Whatipu wharf, you could once see the outline of the tracks in rotting sleepers. On the south rocks the remains of the bolts that held the sleepers cemented into the rock by sulphur can still be seen as a reminder of where the tracks once were.

Wally had known this stretch of coast most of his young life, riding, walking and flying over it. As a young man, collecting guests and returning them to the rail station was a daily assignment. As horse and coach and dray and wagon started to give way to motor transport, there was a fascination with the possibility of ease and comfort these machines could provide. In 1905 there were only 570 cars on the roads in New Zealand and none were registered. By 1920 the number of motor vehicles had grown to 50,000 and by 1930 to 120,000. This was the transport of the future and the clever Badhams, proprietors of what was now becoming one of the Auckland region's most exciting and stylish resorts, were keen to ensure their guests were given the best treatment. They invested in a series of motor vehicles that could withstand the mud and slush of the road to Karekare and reduce travelling time. They arranged to pick up guests not only from the station at Glen Eden, but in the years of the growing depression and to ensure a continuing stream of paying guests, Badham Snr and Wally would drive into town, leaving in the dead of night and pick them up from their homes in the wealthy Auckland suburbs of Remuera, Meadowbank and Herne Bay. It was a great service. Winchelsea House was advertised in glossy publications like the popular *Weekly News* and the *Observer*. Advertisements boasted five-star accommodation, table service and a tennis court. Business boomed.

Winchelsea House was the best of three guest-houses on the West Coast. The Bethell family ran a basic house from around 1900, which consisted of sleeping quarters in tents with permanent wooden floors, two detached cottages, and several small bedrooms. Guests were encouraged to bathe in the small Lake Waiatarua. Like the Badhams, all the family cooked for the guests. Accommodation has continued to the present day, with Trude Bethell-Paice, a granddaughter of Pa Bethell, continuing to run Bethells Beach Cottage. At Whatipu in 1890, the Gibbons' mill-house cottages became very pleasant but basic accommodation venues, with a large dining room and the mill quarters were easily renovated to their guests' satisfaction. Fishing was the biggest attraction; the largest snapper ever

The Weekly News advert, 14 October 1940.

caught in New Zealand was caught here by a guest in the 1930s. Food for all three guest-houses was sourced in the ranges or grown on the property and included pigs, sheep, eggs and milk and a massive vegetable garden, which kept the kitchens and the tables well supplied.

There was one major social change taking place during the 1930s as New Zealand moved towards the Great Depression. The Badham enterprise realised it was going to become difficult to find the richer paying guests who had the time and the money to take a weekend, Christmas or Easter sojourn on the West Coast. In 1931 civil service wages were cut by 10% and in 1932 opposition spokesman and later prime minister, Peter Fraser, stated that New Zealand was in danger of drowning; drown it certainly did. In 1933, 51,000 men were registered as unemployed. 'The Slump' continued into some of the bleakest years in New Zealand's history. Karekare regulars were affluent, exciting and the A-listers of the day. They could afford what many could not; a coastal holiday. There was also a culture change taking place, influenced by magazines and film. It had a lot to do with sex, grooming and obtaining a tan. Beach culture moved quickly; gone were the stringent neck-to-knee costumes of the 1920s and on the beach people now wore more comfortable and practical swimming attire. A younger generation learned to swim, surf and enjoy the thrill of the swan-dive. Swimming was suddenly in fashion so the black sands of the West Coast became a courting ground. Water, sea and surf were a free and available attraction. No matter how difficult your life was, a Nivea tan and a beach towel solved everything.

In his Royal Bentley, the Governor-General and his staff came to picnic and the Duke of York visited Piha. The West Coast was wild; you could surf — not the kind of surfing we see today, but using a large flat piece of wood that would be pushed in front of the swimmer to catch rather small waves. The boarding house kept a ready supply of boards for guests. Wally remembered rescues, disasters, people swept out, drownings and remarkable saves, in particular the amazing rescue of a young nurse, Hazel Bentham, in February 1935, who was saved by a seaplane after she had been swept out to sea in a rip. Plucked from the water after spending three hours afloat drifting towards Piha, her rescue is the first recorded successful air–sea rescue in the world. From this rescue a local surf club was formed and Dudley Badham Snr was their sponsor, coach and team manager. He was very popular and arranged for the fledgling club to set up in the tennis changing sheds. When these burned down old Mrs Farley gave the club her last beach section to build their first clubhouse.

Aviation was a lifelong passion for Wally Badham. His personal courage and flying ability seemed to be quite remarkable because the aircraft he learned to fly in, and then fly solo over Karekare, were not easy machines to handle. His passion for flying remained all his life. Along the way he met some of New Zealand's most important aviation pioneers such as D.M. Allen and others who formed the basis of the air services for World War II when their small planes were commandeered into service.

When Wally and I finally arrived at the coast and drove onto the current Winchelsea House lawn, Wally was stunned by its transformation. Dorothy Butler, the present owner, and her family had restored the house and completed additions in the style of the Murdoch era. Wally toured the place, amazed and enthralled that it was both old yet new; I would have done anything to have taken Wally down on to the beach but as the day grew longer his energy flagged. It was time to return him to his residence.

Our trip was his last pilgrimage to Karekare and although half a century had gone by, I think he was pleased Karekare had kept the essence he remembered it having during his youth. Change had not destroyed it. Suburbia had not reached out its destructive hand. The pohutukawa trees that lined the road when he was a boy have continued to flourish; the streams and the roads have been melded into the landscape of his youth. I told him that we would publish his manuscript in the years ahead.

Wally did not live a happy life after the Karekare years. Much went wrong in the life of this young, enterprising and likeable man. His marriage was not happy and as he aged he became estranged from his family, drifting into a lonely decline. Those people who listened to his jokes and his Karekare tales he liked, to others he was silent. This was how I came into his life — to listen and help tell his tale.

The Iron-Bound Coast is rich in its history of the landscape; there is a cast of locals and visitors and a cross-section of hermits and early settlers; pioneers who lived a private and often secret existence in the Ranges, refugees from society and the Depression, who made their own way in what must have been trying circumstances. They had no power, water or basic services and were often without any medical help. Despite limited communication with the outside world, they thrived, raising children, writing books, painting and cooking. The Ranges drew and nurtured these individuals and Wally clearly enjoyed their company and their personal stories.

When Wally gave me his manuscript, I realised it is truly a rich gem, a legacy of not only remote Karekare beach, but a grand story of this country. He speaks in a voice that reflects the time; a time that is now rapidly fading in memory and people. Working closely with his descendants, we have gathered together Wally's original papers and reproduced them so other readers may hear his voice.

Before he died, Wally had managed to carefully select images from the family photo album to accompany his hand-written manuscript. The title, *The Iron-Bound Coast*, is from the bush railway that ran from Karekare to Whatipu, images of which are prevalent on the covers of Wally's original diaries.

This volume is, in his own words, Wally's story.

Dedication
Wally Badham

This book is a descriptive account of my life, with brief glimpses of earlier days, as told to me by my grandparents, parents and the early settlers of the coast.

It is dedicated to my niece Raewyn who, after returning from Austria, was interested in my early photos and talks of the early days on the West Coast. The period I remember very well are the years 1921 to 1950 while living at Karekare Beach. My earliest memories are of 1918 when the bush-tram engine was running between Karekare and Whatipu. In the early years I was taken out to the coast on several excursions from my home at Ethel Street, Mt Albert. I was christened in the drawing room of Winchelsea House exactly 52 years to the day after the sinking of the HMS *Orpheus* on the Manukau Bar.

My forebears

Mr Charles Thomas Dale Farley and Mrs Maria Mary Farley — my maternal grandparents

Mr Charles Thomas Dale Farley was born in Byford, Herefordshire. At the time he left for New Zealand he was living at St Catherine Villa, Bromyard Road, Worcester, which was nearly opposite the Sandpits Inn, now called The Bedwardine.

I have in my possession a complete catalogue of the two-day auction that was held there. It was on Tuesday and Wednesday, March 14 and 15, 1882. Among the many very interesting things to go under the hammer was a valuable oleograph, 'The Last Moments of Mary Queen of Scots'. This and other items are too numerous to describe here, but it will be of interest that the auction was held by Everill and Day, Auctioneer and Estate Agents of 51 Forgate Street, Worcester. The house premises were then to be let.

Before deciding to leave England, my grandparents had considered two countries: Tasmania, Australia and New Zealand. After obtaining all the information they could about the two countries, they decided that New Zealand would be the most suitable place. They arrived about May 1882. They landed in Auckland and lived on the North Shore then at Wairoa South (Clevedon), before moving to Mt Albert to farm in 1887. With Mr Henry Reynold, they established the first dairy factory in the North Island (and the second in New Zealand) at Pukekura, near Cambridge.

A few years later my grandfather was sent by the government to teach the Italians to make butter. He did not like the country and after completion of the contract returned to Auckland and continued farming at Mt Albert. There were frequent trips to (the late) Mr Henry Reynold's farm at Newstead and other farms in the Waikato. This pattern continued right up till 1900. Then came quite a dramatic change.

While talking one day with a group of men about farming and cattle,

Mr Charles Thomas Dale Farley.

Maybe the first photograph of Karekare, produced from a very early glass plate from 1896. The Murdoch girls walk down what is now Watchman Road.

my grandfather was told of a Mr Jack Bethell who had an interesting farm on the West Coast at Te Henga. Jack/John (Pa) Neale Bethell was a farmer, butcher and a miller (1856–1943). A few days later he met Mr Bethell, who had come to town on business. They talked for quite a while and Mr Bethell invited him to come out and see the place, which he had bought in 1886.

I was told the name Te Henga was thought up by Mr Bethell to name a boarding house that he later had at the beach. It was not a proper Maori name, but bits of two names meaning an eating or meeting place.

A week or two later Grandfather had the chance to make the trip out to Te Henga. He was so taken with the wild coast that Mr Bethell said to him, 'Well if you really like the coast, there is a place called Karekare further down that is for sale.' The property at Karekare was owned by Mr Charles Murdoch, who came up from Dunedin in 1879 to manage the mill at Whatipu for Guthrie and Lanark.

Before going back to my grandfather and Mr Bethell, I will refer to another item of interest from 1875. It will give you an idea of the prices then.

Saturday July 19, 1875

FOR SALE, land between Bombay and Pokeno near to the railway station and Great South Rd. There is a small slab house upon the farm and 15 acres cleared and in grass. Price 37s 6d per acre.

FOR SALE a pretty suburban residence near the Royal Oak Hotel, Epsom. There are 5 rooms together with coach house, stabling and a cowshed and 5 acres rich volcanic soil, also a garden and orchard. Price 700 pounds.

Joseph Moses: Leviathan Clothing Establishment. On receipt of 5 pounds I will at once forward, to any town in New Zealand, the following goods:
- one pair of tweed trousers, shrunk and suited for the saddle
- one pair best mole skin trousers
- one superior black cloth
- all wool crinoline shirts
- New Zealand flax shirts
- pairs strong cotton socks
- strong elastic belt
- white handkerchiefs

Mr Farley and Mr Bethell had now decided that the girls should ride out and see Mr Murdoch. They were Miss Zoe Farley (later to become my mother) and Miss Jessie Bethell. Zoe Farley was 11 at the time and Jessie Bethell was a bit older.

They set off early one morning, going through the Simla Track and down through Anawhata and over Whites Hill into Piha. (Years later, in May 1942, I was camped just below Simla on the edge of the road while acting

The mill at Whatipu

The mill had originally been started by Mr Nicholas Gibbons in 1867 and was driven by a water wheel, said to be about 20 feet in diameter and 4 feet wide.

This quiet locality became a scene of excitement with the arrival of the iron horse or road steamer. Mr R.P. Gibbons, with his usual enterprise, had purchased it from the government with the idea of working it along the beach to haul timber from the Pararaha Valley sawmill to the wharf at Whatipu. It left Onehunga on board a large punt that was towed down the Manukau by a cutter to Huia Creek and from there to Whatipu by rowing boats.

It was hauled up to the beach, strong planks were put over the side to form a ramp and the iron stranger steamed itself ashore amid cheers from the little community. It was intended to haul 8–10,000 feet of timber behind, but I do not know if it was a success.

The kauri in the Pararaha was milled through the 1870s by Captain William Foote. Unfortunately fire swept through the valley in 1881 and destroyed all the standing trees and later the mill itself burned down.

Some of the machinery from this mill was taken to Karekare and Mr Murdoch was sent there to manage that mill. The big boiler was put on one of the timber trucks and they set out to take it to Karekare with the engine, but it was too big to go through the Pararaha tunnel. They then rolled it off and left it there; it is still there today, slowly rusting through the years from 1883.

In 1933 I was fortunate enough to meet Captain Foote. He had worked at Pararaha, Whatipu and Huia and had come back to Karekare for the day to have a look at the valley again and see what changes had taken place. I had quite a long talk with him and he told me a good many things about the early days and the great kauri forests of the Waitakere Ranges.

I remember how we stood in the front of the powerhouse as we talked. Looking out to sea he kept saying, 'Just look at the height of the sand-hills, it was not like that in the seventies.'

The home of John and Silas Shaw, 1878. Behind is Clear Hill Gully, and just in front, but out of the picture, is the Norfolk pine that was planted in memory of the little girl who drowned in the creek.

The Murdochs pick blackberries sold by the Oratia Nursery as a 'special and rare fruit' in 1891.

The Farley family, image dated around 1900. From left to right. Back: Noel, Charles Jnr, Wallace, Marjorie. Middle: Mary Mitchell (Maria's aunt), Charles, Maria. Front: Zoe (Wally Badham's mother), Laurence.

as a scout for the Army during the Jap scare.) Mr Murdoch put them up for the night and they returned the next day with the information Mr Farley wanted. A few days later they all drove out in the coach to look the place over and decided to buy it.

They were told by Mr Murdoch that after the mill closed down he remained on and farmed the land he had bought from John and Silas Shaw. The Shaws had farmed the valley through the 1870s and when they sold to Murdoch they moved to Oratia. Sadly, the youngest of the Murdoch's nine children drowned in Karekare Stream. The child was buried nearby.

It was now time for the Murdochs to leave and move to Auckland where they set up business as wheelwrights and wood turners.

With the Farleys settled in, Karekare was to see yet another change, but not a sale this time. When they left England to come out, the family doctor, Dr Stopwood, came with them. It was not long before he came out to have a look at the place and before the

Farleys knew what was about to happen, the doctor was sending people out to them for a rest and a change from the city.

So the house now became a boarding house and from then was known as Winchelsea House. The name was chosen because my grandmother lived in Winchelsea, England, for a time before she met Mr Farley. Grandfather was so well known that he received a letter from England in 1903, addressed simply to:

> Mr C.T.D. Farley
> Karekare
> Waikumiti
> Near Auckland

The boarding house and farm was a lot of hard work from the year 1900 on and grandfather managed them both for 25 years. He died on 9 March 1926 at the home of his daughter, my Aunt Madge, who lived in Folk Street, New Lynn.

My grandmother, Mrs Maria Mary Farley, was Miss Maria Withersby before she married. She was born in Ipswich, Suffolk, in 1857. She had six children: Charlie, Wally, Laurie, Noel, Marjorie and Zoe. Charlie and Wally were born in England and the others here in Auckland.

Grandmother had a hard time of it at Mt Albert with the six children, but it became harder for a good many years after the move to Karekare.

Those were the coach days and with the boarding house now going

The four-horse coach on its way to the coast near Lone Kauri, driven by John Harry Wilkins in 1900. In the Depression years of the 1930s I drove the service car over this same area, sometimes three trips a day, in and out of Auckland.

The pigeon post

The original 'pigeon gram' that announced the news of the death of Queen Victoria to Great Barrier in less than an hour is in the possession of Mr H.W.G. McFarlane of Hamilton. His father, the late Mr Tom McFarlane, surveyed the Barrier Islands and much of Coromandel Peninsula. The pigeon gram had been in papers left by the late Mrs Constance McFarlane, a member of the Osborne family, who also had a long association with the Barrier.

The pigeon post reported from 1896–1908. Each bird carried five messages written on rice paper. Each message cost a shilling to send. They were franked with what may be the world's first airmail stamps, issued ten years before the first mail plane landed at Saint Nazaire from Paris.

The stamps were printed by the Observer printing works in Auckland and depicted a pigeon holding an envelope in its beak with the words, 'Special Post' above it.

The pigeon post was started by Mr Walter Fricker and the agent at the Barrier end, a Miss Springhall. Later Mr Holden Howie of Auckland took over the loft of 90 birds in Newton Road. The Motor Copper Syndicate at the Hen and Chickens Islands and the Kauri Timber Co. used the service.

The two most famous birds were Teuria and Velocity and their pictures are on the pigeon gram. Velocity held the Australian and New Zealand record of 78 miles an hour, the distance from the Barrier to Auckland in 50 minutes.

ABOVE The old home on the corner of McLeans Road and New North Road, Mt. Albert, in 1890.

LEFT Grandfather Charles Farley with my brother, John Badham, 1921.

BELOW Mrs Maria Mary Farley.

A coach leaves Karekare to return guests to the Glen Eden Station, a five-hour trip.

Arthur Farley feeding the calves and the lambs, 1902.

people had to make the five-hour trip from Waikumete (as it was called then). The name 'Glen Eden' sprang from the number of English emigrants who settled in the area. Waikumete was a bit of a tongue twister; there was also the fear that mail might end up in the dead letterbox. I remember the time of the change very well.

The coach left Karekare at 5 a.m. This meant getting up at 4 a.m. to get the horses in and have them hard fed before the journey. Breakfast was at 4.30 a.m. and the coach left at 5 and took five hours to get to Waikumete. The horses were then given a two-hour spell before the return trip, arriving back at the coast at 5 p.m. At different times the coach was driven by Mr Harry Wilkins, Mr Gill Wood and Mr Wally Farley.

After the coach left Karekare, the cows had to be milked. There was no separator in those days, so the milk had to be left overnight in large milk pans. It was Mrs Farley's job to skim the cream off the next morning and put it aside for butter-making. This was done in a churn turned by hand.

There was no telephone so carrier pigeons were kept. Their loft was on the side of the stable. Each time the coach left, several of these birds were also taken in a box. If there were any unexpected arrivals getting off the train at Waikumete, a message was attached to the leg of one of the birds and it was let go. In ten minutes it would arrive through the trapdoor in the loft and be promptly received. Those at home always kept a lookout for any incoming pigeons so they knew exactly how many would arrive on the coach for dinner.

> I can remember an earlier event told to me by my mother. It was the winter of 1902 and the four-horse coach left as usual at 5 a.m. It was pitch dark and they could not see very well, so the driver left it to the horses to make the turn in the pitch dark after they got over the bridge. The next thing they knew was all being thrown out in a heap; the leader did not turn soon enough and went up the bank of the Clear Hill. When Wally Farley realised where they were he pulled them round and over the coach went. Laurie Farley, who was one of the passengers, was very indignant at the mud on his trousers and hat all squashed in and kept saying to Wally, 'You must have known where you were, surely to goodness?'

My forebears 23

Joe

One evening, as they were finishing dinner, a man walked in with a swag on his back and asked if there was a job to be had. Mr Farley asked him what he could do and he said, 'Most anything, but I am a wood cutter.' As they wanted some more ti-tree cut for firewood, he looked like the answer. The man was given a meal and shown to a room for the night. He said his name was Joe.

Now, Mr Farley always fed the fowls; he had about a hundred of them, including a lot of Guinea fowl. As he had to go into town the next day and the coach left before it was daylight, he asked Joe if he would feed the fowls before going in to the bush. The coach had no sooner left than there was an awful commotion. Everyone rushed outside to see what was wrong. There was Joe using a long ti-tree pole to prod the fowls out of the pohutukawa trees. Mrs Farley said, 'What on earth are you doing?' and Joe replied, 'Well Mrs, the boss is up and it's time they were.' It was quite a job to get them to settle down as it was not yet daylight — the ground was covered with feathers.

Mr Laurie Farley, my uncle, said, 'You can go to the bush, Joe, and we will feed them later.' So Joe picked up his pikau and set off in haste. (A pikau is a sugar bag with a short rope tied to the two bottom corners. A half hitch was then put in so it could be carried on your back.) Joe had what he called a slush light, a small tin of mutton fat with an old sock twisted up and stuck in the middle for a wick. This, he claimed, kept the mosquitoes away (and incidentally everyone else).

Joe would have home-made bread for his lunch, as it was all home-made in those days. He would also have a small leg of lamb and a half-pound of butter.

Joe said that he only had one religion and that was, 'Six days shalt thou labour and on the seventh thou shalt wash and tailor,'; he did all his washing and mending on Sunday. Joe was a terrific worker and did not believe that 'manual labour was a Spaniard.' The Farleys soon found out that as well as his religion he got up with the birds and went to bed with the birds.

Fred Farley feeding the fowls.

Mrs Farley was famous for her cooking, particularly pastry, which she made with home-made butter. I can always remember her saying, you can't make good pastry if you are skimpy with the butter. My grandmother always insisted on the meals being punctual and that is the way it was through the coaching days on the coast.

I will now tell of an amusing incident that took place one day when Mrs Farley discovered she was out of yeast. There were some schoolboys staying out there for a few days and they had all gone fishing but one. This

Mrs Farley with two cattle dogs and a kitten, 1901.

The old home. The stable and the pigeon loft are hidden by the branch of the pohutukawa tree.

boy was keen to learn to ride and was getting on quite well, so she thought, 'Here is the answer, I will get him to ride to Whatipu and get some yeast from Mrs Gibbons.' The boy was delighted to go; the horse they gave him was called Jack McLuskey and was picked because he was reliable. There was only one fault with him, he could not stand another horse in front of him but as he was to be on his own it was thought to be no problem. They reached Whatipu safely and started on the return trip. They were about half a mile from Pararaha when another horseman suddenly appeared on top of a sand-hill. Old Jack saw him, started to jig first on one leg and then on the other, next it was a canter and then a hard gallop.

In the meantime the yeast was starting to fizz and the boy, desperately clutching the bottle with one hand and hauling on the bridle with the other, now had a problem. The climax soon came with a loud bang, away flew the cork ... and the horse as well. They thundered down on the other horseman and Old Jack, having caught up, now came to a sudden stop and flung the boy onto the sand in front of the other horse.

This new rider was one of the Gibbons boys from Whatipu who had been out having a look at some cattle in the Pararaha. When he was told about the yeast he said, 'Well, you had better come back with me and get some more.' This the boy did and, not taking any more chances, he walked all the way back, leading the horse and clutching the bottle of yeast as if it was gold.

Another amusing incident took place not long after. The victim this time was Mrs Farley. They had quite a number of sheep on the property and now and again lambs had been reared on the bottle. One was a ram called Brandy; he was starting to get a bit playful. For quite a while they had all been going down to the beach for a paddle in the surf before going to bed. Someone had said that this ram would go for you and Mrs Farley said, 'It's nonsense, he never goes for me.'

This particular evening she was with them and they had to cross a plank over the creek on to the sandhill. The lambs could be seen grazing not far away and one of the guests said, 'Well, you go first then.' Mrs Farley started off and got about halfway over when Brandy looked up and spotted them. He leapt in the air and in a series of bounds came straight for the plank, jumped on it, and butted Mrs Farley into the creek. There was a chorus of, 'I thought he wouldn't go for you!' Brandy seemed to think everyone on the plank was worth two on the bank.

Another evening while on one of these paddling trips, they had stayed out longer than usual and it got dark. One man said, 'I know the way, just follow me.' So they all came after him in single file. Everything was all right for a while, and then suddenly there was a blood-curdling yell from the self-appointed leader. He had brought his toe into violent contact with an iron bolt in a piece of wood embedded in the sand.

Grandmother survived the war years and then after a short illness, died at 6 a.m. on Monday 3 November 1947. So ended a long and colourful life.

Edward Dudley Cust Badham — my father

Edward Dudley Cust Badham's parents were both born in Calcutta, India. E.D.C. Badham's father, Edward Cust Badham, was manager of the Calcutta branch of the South British Fire and Marine Insurance Company of New Zealand for less than two years before he died of tuberculosis in 1889, aged 26.

At the age of five, Edward Jnr was sent to Miss Cocks' school in Goram and later to St Paul's School at Jalapahar, Darjeeling, 7500 feet above sea level. From the school grounds the pupils could look out and across to Tibet. Darjeeling was also served by the narrowest gauge railway line in the world, twisting and turning up into the hills. As a little chap I often listened to my father as he explained it all to me.

Nepal is the home of the Gurkha, a lovely tribe of little hill men, who did so much in World Wars I and II. A Gurkha never takes his knife from the sheath without drawing blood and I remember my father telling me of the

Edward Dudley Cust Badham, 25 July 1912.

Gurkha in battle who made a swipe at his enemy. 'Ha, you have missed,' said the enemy and the Gurkha replied, 'You wait till you nod your head.'

My father had two older brothers and they all attended St Paul's School. George Badham, the eldest, was School Captain in 1903, then came John Badham. George and John emigrated to England and I know little of them except that John did come out to Karekare, some time before I was born.

In the first year Edward was at St Paul's, his father died. Edward Jnr's mother married again to become Mrs G.F. Ross of 3/1 Landsdowne Road, Calcutta. My father left St Paul's School on 27 November 1904, and for five years he worked on a steamer trading up the River Ganges. At the time, he was 300 miles or more from the nearest English settlement.

It was on one of the river trips that he got malaria. After a spell back in Calcutta, the doctor said, 'Take a trip to far-off New Zealand, get away from the East for a while.'

In 1909 my father left for New Zealand with a return ticket that was never used. The family have little information of his whereabouts after arriving in Auckland and up till the time he met Miss Zoe Farley (who later became my mother) at Karekare. We do know that he was on a farm for a while in Ness Valley and also at Te Kuiti in the King Country. He then came back to Auckland and his next job was with the Tramway Company. He had to pay all the motor men and conductors at the Epsom Tram Barn. In those days the trams were run by a private company and they paid the Auckland City Council £500 a year for the right to run and they could show a profit on it.

In 1911 he went with some others out to Karekare Beach for the weekend. There he met Miss Zoe Farley. They used to go riding together from then and she was a good rider, always riding sidesaddle. The trips out for weekends continued right up till the time of the wedding, which was held there in what they called the drawing room. I shall tell of that later when I refer to my mother's life at Mt Albert in 1889 and then of the Karekare days from 1900.

At the time my father started school in 1892, Queen Victoria was Empress of India. I remember him telling me how the Union Jack was kept continually flying over the ruined Residency of Lucknow by day and night, for 90 years.

The sole honour of not lowering the flag at sunset was bestowed by Her Majesty on the Boys' School for their exemplary honour and also as a tribute to those who defended Lucknow in 1857 during 140 days of hell, until relief arrived. The defence of the Residency of Lucknow was one of the epics of the nineteenth century.

This is the early part of my father's life, up until the time of the wedding.

I wrote to my grandmother in later years; I remember my mother saying, 'Write to your grandmother in India'. This was after I had come to live permanently at Karekare in May 1921. I have in my possession an envelope addressed to me by my grandmother, which has been reproduced here. It is date-stamped Darjeeling 23 November 1922, and the head on the stamp is that of King George IV.

Miss Zoe Farley — my mother

My mother was Miss Zoe Farley before her marriage. She was born in Mt Albert on 19 June 1889.

Her early play days seem to have been with the Caughey boys, Marsden and Hughey, who lived close by. From what she told me, they had a bit of a cave in the grounds and could vanish from sight very quickly when playing. One of their favourite tricks was to put something out on the front path about dusk, with a bit of dark twine attached to it. This was then let through a small hole in the hedge to the edge of the cave. A lot of people came past on their way home from work and it was not long before someone thought they had a find, but just as they nearly got to it, whoosh, it was gone.

Race days were always an attraction as the big brakes, with loads of people, came past on the way to the Avondale Racecourse. On one particular day Marsden Caughey threw a rotten egg into a big brake full of people. There was an awful commotion and no one could see where it had come from. It had hit two people, a man and a woman, and they got told to get out. They didn't want to so the argument got worse and so did the smell. Then one of the horses started to play up and they all had to get out; in the meantime more brake loads had come up behind. Those who had got out because of the horse playing up could not get away from the smell, and the two who had been hit kept following them with nowhere else to go. What a mix up. Down in the cave there were some anxious moments as the group hoped the people would all move on. Eventually they did after several had started shouting, 'We will be late for the races.'

With her sister, Madge, Zoe played a lot with the Caughey boys and they seem to have got into quite a lot of mischief at times.

Some of her other playmates were the Spragg boys who also lived close by. I have often heard her talk of Mr Wesley Spragg and how strict he was with them. Wesley Spragg was an Auckland businessman who lived on Mountain Road (Spraggs Bush bears his name). He was a generous donor and promoter of Centennial Park (1940). In 1920 he gave 761 acres of land around Cornwallis and Kaitarakihi on the Manukau to Auckland City.

It was now 1898. One day, Mr Farley was introduced to three Indian Army officers from the Governor-General's Body Guard, who were in Auckland. He invited them out to Mt Albert to stay a few days and they took a fancy to Zoe. When they asked her name and she said, 'Zoe', one of them said that was the name of his mother and that she was a Persian woman. He then took a badge from his tunic and gave it to Zoe, saying, 'As your name is Zoe, the same as my mother, I would like you to have it.'

Miss Zoe Farley.

Madge and Zoe Farley, 1893.

> Star of India 1880
>
> Given to me by Ibna Ali, one of the Governor Generals' Body guard, he marched to 'Kandahar' with Lord Fredrick Roberts, there were 10,000 men in the army, they marched 133 miles. He wore this Star of India on his tunic, during the Siege. He gave me this when I was a little girl at our Mt Albert home. 1898.
>
> Z K Badham

ABOVE The three Indian Army Officers. At centre is Ibna Ali, whose badge was given to me after my grandmother's death.

LEFT Some information about where The Star of India badge came from is provided in this note from Zoe.

Wally Farley, Zoe's brother.

The badge was The Star of India and Ibna Ali had worn it on his tunic when he marched 133 miles with 10,000 men under Lord Frederick Roberts to Kandahar, Afghanistan in 1880. The march was to aid the fort that had been under siege for a while. He wore it all the time, on his tunic, during the march and the siege. It is one of my proud possessions, and I often wore it when my father dressed me up as an Indian boy for fancy dress balls at Karekare in the 1920s.

After the move to Karekare, Zoe settled down to riding and often went pig hunting with her brother, Wally. I remember her telling me of the day they got on to a mob in a clearing and there was several big flax bushes among the short scrub. He told her to get up in one and stay there so that if he got a chance to shoot he would know where she was. A bit later he did take a shot and picked a big boar, which he carried home, while Zoe took

My forebears 29

ABOVE Wally Farley and Arthur White with a wild bull, 1902.

RIGHT Arthur White and Wally Farley, 1901.

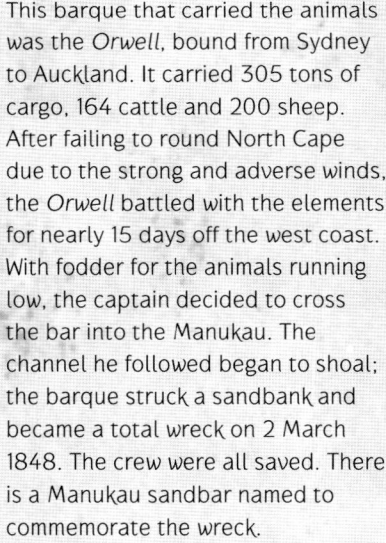

This barque that carried the animals was the *Orwell*, bound from Sydney to Auckland. It carried 305 tons of cargo, 164 cattle and 200 sheep. After failing to round North Cape due to the strong and adverse winds, the *Orwell* battled with the elements for nearly 15 days off the west coast. With fodder for the animals running low, the captain decided to cross the bar into the Manukau. The channel he followed began to shoal; the barque struck a sandbank and became a total wreck on 2 March 1848. The crew were all saved. There is a Manukau sandbar named to commemorate the wreck.

the rifle. He later gave her the tusks, which she mounted and then gave to me a few years before her death.

Mother had many other hunting trips with Wally. I also have some photos of him and Arthur White hunting wild cattle. From 1848 till as late as 1926, the Waitakeres were full of wild cattle. They originally came from a boat that was wrecked on the Manukau Bar and many of them managed to swim ashore to get into the bush at Pararaha.

These hunting trips were necessary because the wild bulls would come out of the bush on a moonlit night, call out from the top of the Clear Hill and then lead the dairy cows off into the bush. When this happened they had to go after them, shoot the wild bull and then begin the job of getting the cows home again. Often there were other wild bulls in the open calling out — getting the cows headed for home and out of the thick bush was quite a job.

About this time electricity came to Karekare; they had it long before Auckland did. The second generator to be imported into New Zealand came to this valley. It was 110 volts and operated right up till July 1933 when we changed over to 230 volts. It was driven by a pelten wheel, which had earlier been used to operate the flax mill.

The water to drive the pelten wheel was diverted from the top of the waterfall and brought along a flume built up on trestles through the bush for about 200 yards. It then fell into a 600-gallon tank and down a 6-inch jarrah pipe with a drop of 180 feet to the powerhouse below. This gave a

The flax mill

I knew little of the flax mill but think it operated in Murdoch's time. All I know is the method they used to get the flax down from the hills. This was to tie the bundle with a flax band at each end. Two wire hooks were used; one end was placed under the load and the other was a piece of light gauge fencing wire, which had been strung from the bottom of the hill to the loading point. I used the same method to get ti-tree firewood down from the hills. I would bury a piece of wood and have about eight feet of wire sticking out of the ground. A spring was then attached to the wire to go up the hill, made fast at either end. I then pulled it tight with a Donald wire strainer and took the slack round a good solid tree. This way, a lot of wood could be taken down in a day.

The Mill Valley (1907) with the small waterfall on the left and part of the powerhouse and sheering shed on the right. The kauri paling fence is typical of the time.

The waterfall and flume leading into the bush. This image was taken from the top of the Cave Rock; I am in the foreground.

My forebears 31

A classic shot of Winchelsea House taken from Clear Hill. The kitchen and dining room are behind the guest wing; at the rear are the stables.

pressure of 80 pounds to the square inch and delivered about 15 horsepower with a full head of water.

There were several sized nozzles that could be used according to the amount of water available. They were made of brass, the big one for the winter and the small ones for the summer.

The jarrah pipes came from Western Australia and were 16-feet long, painted with a tar coating with a wooden collar to go over each joint. Guests to Winchelsea House now had electric light in the bedrooms, while back in Auckland the moths continued to fly into the lamps.

Mother now had a chance to do plenty of riding and a good horse trainer, Bill McMaster, had come out and decided the beach would be a grand place to train his horses. I remember how mother used to tell me of the horse called Clive that she rode every day before the races. On the day he was to race she went along with him to watch and was very excited when he came in first and paid £10.

She used to ride the different horses quite a lot and one day Bill told her to take them into the surf as it was good for their legs. A few days after she had started getting them into the surf, a man and his wife came out with a flash gig and stylish horse. Over dinner that night, McMaster said he had been having his horses taken in the surf as it was good for their legs, so the visitor decided to do the same for his horse the next day.

There were about 20 people staying in the house at the time and it was high tide about 5 p.m. that day. Dinner was always at a quarter to six and they had all gone down to the beach for a paddle. Not long after they had

My mother on one of the horses she loved to ride.

gone, this chap put a halter on his horse and followed them down. He rolled his trousers up and tried to get the animal to go in, but the waves frightened it and it refused to go. So he thought he would wait till all the people had gone up for dinner then he would strip off and make the horse go in. After the people had all gone and he had given them time to get up to the house, he started to get the plan into effect. Having placed his clothes in a heap on the beach, he grabbed the halter and jumped on. The horse went out a few yards and came back. He then made it turn around and dug his heels into the horse, it went out a bit further. Just then an extra big wave came and the horse took fright, turned, and bolted for home. With just the halter, the visitor did not have much control over the animal as it thundered up the edge of the creek below The Watchman. He thought of jumping off but there was driftwood all along his path of flight. The next thing he knew the horse clattered over the middle bridge in front of the powerhouse, then came the big bridge in front of the boarding house and up to the stable, where it stopped, suddenly flinging him off.

The middle bridge, 1904.

Now, everyone was at dinner when they heard the clatter of horse's hooves over the two bridges and they threw the chairs back in a wild rush to get out and see who this crazy horseman was.

The first of the guests got to the lawn just as the horseman thundered past and was then thrown off his ride. In the middle of the uproar the visitor picked himself up and dived into the stable. Here he stayed while someone rushed off down the beach to get his clothes. With no long hair everyone was convinced it was not Lady Godiva!

The Point, with Mt Zion in the distance. Sugar Loaf Rock is in the foreground.

About a week later the visitor was down in Dunedin and the bush telegraph had been at work. He was told, 'I hear you have been imitating Lady Godiva at Karekare.' Was it a carrier pigeon or tapping on the tree trunks?

At the time Mr Farley bought Karekare in 1900, Zion Hill and Sandringham Valley stretched from the road to the north point. This was originally owned by Mr Abel Lovett, who had it left to him by a Norwegian named Pedersen, who died about 1894. Pedersen built a place of kauri palings just near the

My forebears 33

The view from the top of Mt Zion looking south over Pararaha to Windy Point and Whatipu. The Pararaha tunnel is in the dip and the mill workers' cottages are just beyond, 1904.

Some of the Farley family, 1904. From left: Arthur White, Wally Farley, Zoe Farley, Aunt Madge, Mrs Farley, Laurie and Mrs Sugget. I am not sure who the other person is.

end of the valley below the Black Rock, as I called it. My mother once told me that Pedersen carried a Donver stove up from the valley on his back and I can just imagine what a job that must have been.

He also kept his cattle in stalls and went out and cut food for them, just like they do in Norway. This is what it was like in the 1870s, with him farming Karekare Point and John and Silas Shaw in the Sandringham Valley.

I often looked at the remains of Pedersen's old home when I was getting the cows in. It gradually rotted away and the ti-tree, or manuka, closed in so that today there is nothing to indicate that a home once stood there.

I did not know Mr Pedersen but I knew Mr Abel Lovett and often saw him at Karekare when I was at school. He farmed the Point for a good many years after Mr Pedersen died and then, about 1902, sold it to Mr Farley for £500. My grandfather now owned both sides of the valley, 500 acres all told, and was the first one to do so.

On the south side of the new property was the high cliff, Mt Zion at 900 feet. The boundary fence was just beyond. Between Karekare and Pararaha Valley was purchased by Mr and Mrs Sugget shortly after Mr Farley purchased the Karekare house and farm.

The wedding

My father-to-be had been going out to Karekare each weekend after his first trip when he met Miss Zoe Farley, who was to become my mother. They were married on 27 May, 1914.

All the guests left town and journeyed to Karekare by coach, where at Winchelsea House they were met by Zoe's parents, Mr and Mrs Farley. After a most appetising tea, hosts and guests adjourned to the hall nearby and a merry dance took place, a programme of musical items being gone through in the drawing room of the house. The following morning, at

The bridal group on the middle bridge in front of the powerhouse. The bridesmaid was Miss Edith Farley, who was a cousin. The best man was Mr Culley Richardson.

10 o'clock, the wedding party and guests assembled in the drawing room and joined in singing the bridal hymn, after which the Rev. Mr Gatman united the happy couple. Mr Farley gave away his daughter who was dressed in a robe of white embroidered silk and wearing her mother's wedding veil attached to a wreath of orange blossom, and carrying a bridal bouquet. The bridesmaid, Miss Edith Farley, was a cousin and wore a pretty white silk dress and cerise hair bandeau and carried an appropriate bouquet. The best man, Mr Culley Richardson, was a school teacher for the mill workers' children at Piha.

Following the wedding ceremony an elaborate breakfast was provided in the hall and the usual toasts were proposed and honoured. After which Mr F. Wiseman photographed the bridal pair, also the guests, some of the photos being taken under the pohutukawa tree and others by the stream. Mr and Mrs Badham then left on their honeymoon tour, the bride costumed in black velvet and wearing a black beaver hat with white wings.

Mrs Farley, the bride's mother, wore an elegant black gown and white feather boa; Mrs L. Farley, black velvet with Maltese collar and cuffs; Mrs Wallace Farley, cream corded silk; Mrs Reardon, rose shot silk; Mrs Sinclair, black silk with ecru trimmings; Mrs Frank Wiseman, rose silk, overdress of rose with white spots; Mrs Wilkins, white satin, overdress of black chiffon; Miss Haddon, white voile; Mrs Qualtrough, grey costume; Mrs Eyre, black and white striped silk, black lace trimmings; Mrs Easton, navy costume; Mrs Johnston, cream and blue voile and Winifred and Elfreda Eyre, cream voile frocks.

One of the wedding guests admires the bush.

The guests in front of the dance hall after the wedding breakfast. The two little girls in front are Winifred and Elfreda Eyre. Just behind them are Mr and Mrs Farley (Snr), Mrs Farley with white feather boa. Behind her are Mr and Mrs Sinclair, the bride and bridegroom, Reverend Gatman and Edith Farley. I am unable to name all of the rest of the group.

The dance hall, 1924.

Winifred and Elfreda Eyre with their mother by the cottage below Cave Rock. The cottage was later owned by my parents in 1925, along with three-quarters of an acre in the shape of a triangle that ran up to a point just below Cave Rock. The new road now goes right through the middle of this land. Wally Farley also lived here for a number of years and was living in it in 1921 when I came to live at Karekare. I can remember how in early 1923 I helped his children (my cousins) to carry many of the small things when he moved to the cottage by the mill.

The land before the cottage was built, 1896.

The same land with Wally Farley's cottage, 1936.

Karekare characters and recollections

Bill Stokes and his bullock team

Mr Bill Stokes was a very good bullock driver and it was said he had never been known to swear at the animals and they would do anything for him.

To see a team in action was a very interesting sight. Each bullock knew its name and it only needed the driver, who walked beside the team with a long whip, to call out the bullock's name and crack his whip over it to make it put mass effort into the pull.

To train a fresh bullock the animal would be yoked alongside a trained bullock and after it had done its best to escape from the wooden yoke that connected it to its mate, it would settle down and become a docile member of the team.

One day a big boiler rolled off one of the trucks and went down into the paddock in front of the house. My mother told me how she watched Bill Stokes' bullocks going straight up the Clear Hill with the leaders down on their knees as they strained to pull it back onto the road.

Bill Stokes had one fault though. He could tell the biggest yarn out and had told them so often that he really believed them.

For a time when Dr Raynor had the mill they had six horse teams pulling the timber around Karekare Point to the huge timber yard at the

Karekare Point with Mt Zion at left and Pararaha and Windy Point in the distance, 1910.

Mr Jack Bendall and his bullock team at Waitakere, 1900.

mouth of the Pararaha Valley entrance. Well, Bill Stokes was driving one of these wagons one day and he told them when he got to the Karekare Point there was still a bit of water around it, about 18 inches or so, and after the waves went back he put the horses into it. About halfway round, the wagon suddenly stopped, and though the horses strained every ounce they could not move it. As soon as the waves went back he jumped down to have a look and found a big snapper had snagged the wheel.

Another one of his yarns was that one day he hooked a big eel in the creek using a shark hook and a chain. He tried for about half an hour to get it out and went and got two of his bullocks and after a struggle they pulled it out.

Another time when six-horse teams were being used to haul timber to Whatipu, one of the wagons got stuck in the soft sands and two men were beating the horses with bits of timber. They had no hope of pulling it out and Bill Stokes, who saw them, got his bullock whip and said he would put it round them if they did not unload the wagon. One look at him and they did.

Just where the bridge is at the foot of the Karekare cutting and going straight up the slope is Stokes' old bullock road, all overgrown like the other old landmarks in the valley.

I did not know Bill Stokes, but I knew Jack Bendall. Mr Jack Bendall was Bill Stokes' one equal when it came to running a bullock team. I often called into Jack's place during 1930s, which was just below Scenic Drive where it joins the West Coast Road. Bendall Creek flows from the old water catchment area down a small waterfall then under Scenic Drive and falls steeply into the Oratia Valley through Waiatarua.

Mr and Mrs Cameron Johnson

Mr Cameron Johnson was an artist and came to Karekare just after Mr Farley settled there in 1900. They lived for quite a while in a nikau whare [house] at the Cutting Creek built by Moffat and Ru Byles. They were experts at this like the old-time Maoris. The whare was snug and comfortable all through the winter and not a drop of rain came in. Mr Johnson did many fine paintings of the valley and fishing rocks, but these were all sold with the place in 1950.

A sketch of Cutter Rock made by Mr Cameron Johnson as he was horse riding with Zoe Farley one evening. The sketch was given to me by my uncle, Laurie Farley, just after the war.

Two images of Cutting Creek near the nikau whare, 1907. From left: Laurie Farley, Mrs Sugget, Mrs Eyre and Mrs Johnson and friends.

Karekare characters and recollections

Essie Johnson's painting of the creek and Paratahi Island, 1905.

This rock is known as Cutter Rock because it was near here that the cutter, from HMS *Orpheus*, wrecked on the Manukau Bar at 2 p.m. It was said to be carrying bullion, which is said to be still buried in the sand near the rock.

After they had been at the coast a few years, the Johnsons had some money left to them so they took a trip back to England. Like many others they returned broke and had to start all over again.

Dr and Mrs Tracy Inglis

Dr and Mrs Tracy Inglis also visited Karekare quite a lot. The doctor was very keen on fishing and, like Dr Stopwood, was always sending people out for a rest.

It was on one of his visits that a boy got into difficulties in the surf and it was just lunchtime. Someone burst in and said there was a boy drowning in the surf and once again the chairs flew back and there was a mad rush for the beach.

Now there was another handyman working for them, called Harry. He had gone to the smokehouse to see how the fish was getting on. He knew nothing about the boy in the surf and Mrs Jones rushed up to him as he came back with a tray of fish. She handed him a man's hat and said, 'Quick, run after Mr Jones, he has rushed off down the beach without his hat and I am afraid he will get sunstroke.' Harry's first thought was that he must have gone off his head and he did not like the idea of going after him. The boy was rescued, Mr Jones survived, and Harry stayed with the fish.

Dr Stockwell

A little way past the Karekare turn-off was a house built by Dr Stockwell in 1889. I often passed it riding to Piha. In 1927 I rode past on my way to Piha to get a Dr Redpath to come and have a look at a swelling in my mother's hand. It was on the wrist and had been caused by shelling maize on the farm at Stanmore Bay. He knew what to do and got it fixed for her.

Dr Stockwell was the first one to own Piha — the area had previously been set aside as a nature reserve about 1851 and remained so for a good many years until he purchased it. Several Maori families had resided there at one time and the best known among them is Tauhia Watarauhi. About 1000 acres was owned by the doctor, who had settled there with the Ness and Cowan families in 1868. The stream that flowed through his property he decided to call the Glen Esk, after the one that was near his home in Scotland, but this name has been mixed up a bit with the name 'Ness'.

He later sold to Dr Kenderdine, then for a while Mr Jack (Pa) Bethell

Dr Tracy Inglis (at right) with a friend.

The Piha Valley as Dr Stockwell knew it in 1870.

Haughton's hut

In the days of Pa Bethell, there lived behind the lake, a man named George Haughton. His hut, as was typical of any of those erected in the Ranges, had a huge, open fire place. A suitable log was pushed through from outside and set alight and as it slowly burned away more log was pushed through. Along the two sides of the chimney were benches where one could either sit and enjoy the warmth or, after causing the fire to smoke, stretch out on and go to sleep and be reasonably free of mosquitoes. Some thought the mosquitoes the lesser of the two evils, but many old-timers spent many pleasant evenings resting by the chimney with the dancing flames sending their flickering light out in to the dark room, while the quiet singing of the old kettle hanging on a chain over the fire mingled with the twittering of the night insects.

farmed the valley until it was bought by Dr Raynor who, after milling the more accessible timber, offered it to the City Council for £14,000 in 1914. The offer was rejected and the New Zealand Government Railway obtained the milling rights. So for a few years this part of the Waitakere Ranges became a hive of activity. The mill finally closed down in 1918.

All I know of Dr Stockwell was told to me by my grandmother, mother and Pa Bethell who I often called in to see in the early 1930s when he lived in retirement just on the city side of the Whau Bridge in Avondale.

Mrs Robinson and the *Weka*

One of the boats that ran between Onehunga and Whatipu was the *Weka* and my mother often spoke of her and told me the following incident. There was a Mrs Robinson and her daughter who had been staying at Whatipu through the winter. She was a very stout woman and had done a lot of needlework and had put it all in baskets to take back in the boat to Onehunga. When the *Weka* arrived she was late, it was very rough and the tide was going out. Mrs Robinson could not get on from the slippery steps with the boat going up and down and pulling away from the wharf. The captain was in a hurry to leave as he had to go straight across to Awhitu and there was about a 20 mile an hour current going through the heads on the outgoing tide. In later years I have often stood on the wharf and watched the *Te Toa* go straight across and with the two engines it took her all her time to hold her own against the current. But back to Mrs Robinson. After a

Right The *Weka* off Whatipu Wharf, 1903.

Below My family at Whatipu wharf, 1927.

The Suggets

The incident I am about to tell now was told to me by my mother and is just about all I know of the Suggets who, as previously mentioned, owned the land between Karekare and Pararaha Valley. One day Zoe, her brother Wally, and Mrs Sugget set off with some supplies to go round to Pararaha in the Konaki sled. A Konaki had two wheels at the rear and a sledge runner or wheel in front. The only access to the Sugget's place was from Pararaha. They had four horses in the harness. Just near the powerhouse someone fired a gun off. The horses took fright and bolted. Wally Farley was thrown out with the reins around his legs and when they reached the sand Zoe decided to jump out. This left Mrs Sugget alone, crouched in the bottom, with the four horses giving full gallop for the beach. A few minutes later one of the wheels struck a small log in the sand and it overturned, flinging her out. At the same time the tracers broke. The horses dashed on down the beach and, as others had seen the incident, they [the horses] got quickly rounded up, while the three counted the bruises.

It was fortunate for Mrs Sugget that she landed in the soft sand; I was told that it was quite a while before she was game to get back into the Konaki.

ABOVE The Konaki on the beach with a gig at Pararaha, 1907.

Abel Lovett's old blue cart in front of the sand-hills, 1896.

few attempts the captain decided there was only one thing to do so swung her and all her baskets of treasures on board with the winch. One basket fell into the water and the daughter flew at him for getting her mother on board like cargo. Sorry, no photo of the event as once again the cameraman got excited and dropped the camera in the water. Mrs Robinson eventually got to Onehunga safely and the basket that fell in the water went to Davy Jones' Locker.

Mr and Mrs Herbert Arthur

Rhoda and Herbert Arthur were frequent visitors to Karekare from 1896 when they first came out on their honeymoon with a tent and a camera in 1936. They returned to photograph their favourite places on their 60th wedding anniversary. They had many trips out by coach with Mr Harry Wilkins between 1896 and 1900, which was four years before my grandfather bought the place. Herbert was very keen on photography and spent a lot of time wandering round selecting spots that took his fancy like Cutting Creek, the Fishing Rocks, The Watchman, Karekare Point, the Six Foot Track (now the new road) and the Pararaha Gorge. Many of these fine photos are included in this book as a tribute to him.

Left Newly-wed Rhoda Arthur is about to get water from the creek.

The beautiful pa site south of Karekare and on the way to Pararaha Valley. This image has been produced from a set of glass plates belonging to Herbert Arthur.

The tramway running in front of The Watchman, 1913.

When Herbert was 69 and Rhonda 67, they returned to their honeymoon sites at Karekare. Herbert again recorded Karekare with his camera.

Herbert Arthur, photographer and lover of Karekare, on his honeymoon in 1897. He took his wife Rhonda and his wooden camera for a 10-day stay.

The boy on Paratahi

Not long after Mrs Robinson's experience, some boys that had been staying at Karekare for the holidays had gone down one afternoon for a swim. One of them had gone out a bit far and got caught in a rip and swept towards Paratahi. He managed to climb on the rocks then found he was faced with the problem of how to get off. In the meantime some of the others had rushed up to the house and given the alarm, so as usual everyone made a dash for the beach and the suggestions of what to do became as plentiful as the seagulls flying overhead. The master plan was to build a raft. So back to the house for a hammer, saw and nails. After about an hour the raft was made and ready to put to sea, but disaster struck again — no-one was game enough to go out in it.

A hot argument soon started as to who should be captain and how to get volunteers for crew. As all volunteers refused to volunteer it now looked as if they must come up with a brainwave to counteract those waves that were holding them back. A quick look around and Mr Laurie Farley was spotted, who had been quietly looking on and no doubt wondering what the outcome would be. At last, an answer they thought. We can remain on the beach and volunteer encouragement, it is safer. So now there was a chorus of, 'You're one of the Farley's, why don't you go out?' He did not intend to be caught off balance and quickly replied that he would not have been stupid enough to be out there and it was not his idea to build the raft. So back to square one and as the tide rose their spirits fell to an all-time low — only to be revived by the appearance of Mr Farley Snr who had not only arrived in time but with the only answer to the problem there could be.

Paratahi Island.

Mr Farley's plan was put into action. He said the only thing to do was for someone to ride to Whatipu and get Mr Bob Gibbons to bring a boat along on the Konaki sled. Late in the afternoon the boat arrived and by this time everyone was on the beach, including all the women who had been spring-cleaning or moving the furniture round.

Mr Gibbons now asked the ladies if they would leave the beach as those going out in the boat would have to strip off or get soaked. They did not want to go as they wished to see if the boat could get out to the rock. Finally he said, 'Well, we can't mess around, if you don't mind neither do I.' So he stripped off with several others, got in the boat and headed out into the surf. They got the boy back, but all got soaked and all he could say was that he had a corker time. Those in the boat thought all is well as they landed in a swell. The ladies now left the beach to get hot drinks for the boat crew.

Winchelsea House.

Jack Lawrence and the early bush days

Mr Jack Lawrence was a bushman in the early days of the kauri mills on the West Coast. There were no mechanical chain-saws or bulldozers and almost everything was done through human effort. The workers were soaked in sweat all day, from head to foot, and their boots were often so filled with sweat that it must have felt and certainly sounded as if they were tramping through a bog.

In these conditions the bushmen worked a 10-hour day and a 58-hour week (including 8 hours on Saturday) for about £3. There were no 10-minute smokos. They had to sharpen their axes in their own time — the only thing that would strike was a dry match. If rain was falling heavily at starting time, 7 a.m., they got a day off with pay. But if it began to rain after they had left camp in the morning, they had to bash on for their full 10 hours.

During the 1920s Jack worked for a while in the bush on Great Barrier Island. It was soon after the wreck off the east coast of the island of the steamer *Wiltshire* on 31 May 1922, and many of the local residents were still enjoying the cargo of whisky that had washed ashore. Some of them were drunk for weeks and the horses and sledges were going night and day in the frantic salvaging of the cargo.

After returning from the Barrier Jack remained in the Huia Valley for many years. He ended up living in retirement at Parau.

Timber milling on the West Coast

The Whatipu Mill

The Whatipu Mill was built in 1867 by the enterprising Nicholas Gibbons, who originated from Nova Scotia, hauled logs to the mill over a horse-hauled wooden rail tramway that continued out across the beach to the shelter of the big rock Paratutui, where the sawn timber was rafted to the Onehunga Wharf.

In 1870, Gibbons was joined by William Foote, a fellow Canadian born in Newfoundland, who established a mill at the mouth of the Pararaha Gorge. From the mill he built a tramway along the edge of the cliffs to meet Gibbons' line at Paratutui, where together they built a good size wharf.

This enterprise worked until 1876 when both mills were leased to Messrs Waller and Garlick, a partnership that was to survive little more than six months. Mr Waller finally gave up in August 1877, leaving both mills to be put up for sale.

By this time large numbers of bush workers were around each mill and over 3000 acres of bush was being worked by them. There still remained about 50,000,000 feet of kauri. In November 1878 both mills and surrounding bush were sold to the Dunedin firm of Guthrie and Lanark for £24,000 and Mr Charles Murdoch was then sent up to act as manager.

Murdoch was born in Scotland in 1850 and brought up in the sawmilling trade of his native land. With his experience he operated both the Whatipu and Pararaha mills with great success until 25 March 1881, when fire swept through the Pararaha Mill and bush, completely destroying it. After this disaster Murdoch decided to move the operation north along the coast to Karekare to set up a new mill just below the Big Cave Rock.

Dressed in their Sunday best, Ebenezer Gibbons and his family pose by a water-driven mill saw used for cutting sleepers for a bush tram-track. The stream runs beside the Whatipu Lodge, which was the mill homestead.

The mouth of the Pararaha Gorge showing the towering cliffs on both sides.

The remains of the tramline near Karekare.

The Guthrie and Larnark engine pushed off the track, subject to the vagaries of the shifting sands.

Opals Pool Mill

The new mill was named the Opals Pool Mill. The Whatipu Mill was closed to provide extra machinery and manpower so the tramway could be extended to the new mill, no mean feat as it involved the blasting and digging of a track around the cliff faces and bridging of many gaps in the cliffs. To work this line Charlie Murdoch obtained an engine that had worked in the Grahamstown and Tararu Tramway at Thames. This engine was the first to be built in New Zealand. It was the work of Fraser and Tinnie of Onehunga in 1872 and it is thought to have been built around a Hornsby underframe traction engine, the design for which first appeared in 1863. For use on the Whatipu tramline it was fitted with a good size tender and a collapsible funnel for working under overhanging rock ledges.

Despite Charles Murdoch's energy in establishing this mill below the Cave Rock, it worked only until 1886. After it was closed the machinery was put up for sale and on purchase it was carried out along the tram for the new owners. A section of the tramway was purchased for a firewood venture in the Huia Valley, but the engine had deteriorated in the salty coastal air and the price they wanted, £75, could not be obtained. The engine was then pushed off the track on to the middle of the beach.

The Piha Mill

The first man to attempt milling of timber at Piha was a well-known and, at the time, successful bush contractor, William Stokes. He started in 1906 with a plan to pull kauri logs out of the Glen Esk Valley and drop them down into Karekare to be milled, but this proved to be very expensive and he was soon in financial difficulty.

My mother told me, that in 1907, a dentist, Dr Raynor, who had the highly successful American Dental Parlour on Queen Street, Auckland, decided to join Stokes. They got a mill at Karekare and cut out the remaining timber while still pursuing the Piha idea but the position improved little.

The National Bank of New Zealand, which was providing the finance, finally demanded a written review of the whole situation from an experienced timber man nominated by the bank. He was Mr Chris Ingram and he reported that the Piha timber would be a workable and profitable proposition provided that the mill was moved to Piha and a suitable route for a railway to Karekare was found.

The mill was moved to Piha and erected at the junction of the Piha and Glen Esk streams so that logs from both water sheds could be driven down the respective streams and delivered to the mill trams.

A bolster-load of sawn timber being lowered down Skids Gully on its way to Karekare and eventually the mill-yard by the hauling engine which is just out of sight at the top of the ridge. The loopman or brakeman stands on the ridge silhouetted against the skyline and watches the bolster descend.

A bolster-load of timber being hauled up the Piha incline to the top of Skids Gully.

Timber milling on the West Coast 51

The incline section of the Piha tramline. The brake station is at the top.

> Windy Point was the scene of other activity in these days and a kauri floor was put down inside and dances took place on Saturday nights. My mother, grandmother and early settlers told me quite a lot about it. They came from Anawhata, Piha, Karekare, Pararaha, Whatipu and Huia. Everyone came on horseback and the horses were put in Gibbons' paddock till after the dance. With the dance over, the ride home commenced and there were as many as 30 or 40 horses and riders on the six-mile stretch of beach. The music was usually supplied by Mr Bob Gibbons on his violin and my mother said the only tune he knew was 'What's the matter with father?' So they got this all night.
>
> The Sandfly Express did not run to the dances, for though it was a dry area then, even with the tide out, it was feared some keen drivers could get off the rails a bit.

The National Bank appointed Chris Ingram as General Manager and Robert Gibbons as Task Manager. These men built a tramway up and over the 900-foot hill separating Piha from Karekare, and on top of this hill placed a large steam hauler to move loads over the three sections of the lines. Loop lines long enough to hold a full bolster and an empty were built at the end of each section. They created a giant roller-coaster coming up from Piha Valley, across the road and then down into the Karekare Valley on a section known as Skids Gully. It was the wonder of the age, a spectacular fall of 4:5:1 gradient up from Piha and 2:5:1 gradient down to the Karekare Mill. A brakeman stood at the top controlling the two fully-laden trollies dropping down to Karekare while another was being pulled up on the other side. Each haul lifted one load; one along the lengthy level centre section and one down into Skids Gully. The load at Karekare was sent to the timber skids and the empties were sent back to Piha. Each load to come up from Piha

ABOVE Sandfly.

LEFT The wharf at Whatipu under Paratutui (The Great Rock). The wharf was built by Nicholas Gibbons and William Foote.

towed two lots of slabs as fuel for the hauler.

The timber deposited at Karekare was, in the early days, transported across the beach, then over the remains of the Whatipu line by nine-horse teams. Karekare Point at this time, I was told, was quite clear of water at high tide but Windy Point could only be crossed at low tide and the position was getting worse with the teams only able to work one load each way at low tide. A good southwesterly gale would to bring all movements to a halt, save for stockpiling at Karekare.

These problems only aggravated the financial situation. The Bank demanded that the overdraft be honoured and it was obvious that timber needed to be kept moving in order to meet expenses. A new wharf was built at Whatipu and work was put in hand to rebuild the tramway and speed up the turn-round of skips. The work was slow and regularly disrupted by the weather but it was eventually

Charlie Cowan aboard Sandfly at Big Cave near Windy Point.

Timber milling on the West Coast   53

completed to Karekare Point and ready to take the engine. At Whatipu wharf there was a turntable to feed a line running off at right angles to some timber stacking yards, also a loop and a siding with an engine shed.

The gauge was 3 feet and the track consisted mainly of 5x2 wooden rails and there was also a mixture of 14-, 21- and 28-pound steel track in various places. The engine they got was a small four-wheel Bugnal locomotive purchased from a Manawatu flax mill and nicknamed 'Sandfly'.

The months of rebuilding and the use of the engine sent timber moving down the coast to Whatipu again and the hauler at the top of Skids Gully kept the Karekare skids filled with sawn timber, but the section across the Karekare beach remained a serious problem.

Teams of bullocks and horses were tried, hauling both wagons and sledges, but neither worked with much success and it became increasingly obvious that the tramway must cross the beach and link the rail heads. By this time management had passed to Hans Peter Knutzen and it was he who undertook the laying of the tramlines across the beach.

Sandfly was the first engine and worked only the Whatipu to Karekare section. The second Karekare engine was bought by Dr Raynor from Herman and Luis Seiferts' flax mill near Foxton. It was built by Bignall and Company, England, to an order from J.J. Niven and Company on 4 December 1906. It was a standard catalogue design and built for a three-foot gauge. After an overhaul in the Newmarket workshop and regauging, it had a 'Sandfly' nameplate put on the smoke-box door. When the mill closed down towards the end of 1918 it was sold to the Makatuka Timber Company of Pakihi and the NZR Raetihi branch line. It was in the cab of this engine that I had the ride from Skids Gully down to the boarding house with the driver Jack Sergeant.

After Dr Raynor sold the Piha property, a Mr Kibble White had it and it was he who started cutting it up into sections. It is now a firm part of the over a quarter-acre, half-gallon, pavlova paradise and I am sad to say that Karekare has gone much the same, only on a smaller scale. The difference is that the high sides of the valley are owned by the Centennial Park Board and it is likely to stay that way.

The tramline crossing the creek on to the beach, which was built under the supervision of Hans Peter Knutzen.

This view from the top of Cave Rock shows the tramline winding around The Watchman.

54　The Iron-Bound Coast

Dr Raynor in a hurry

Back to Dr Raynor again and the six- and nine-horse teams that were used to haul the timber while the tramway was being rebuilt. To go through the Karekare Valley and across the beach, Dr Raynor had to get the consent from Mr Farley, who agreed if the empty wagon returning from Whatipu would bring all his heavy goods free of charge. This consisted of sacks of flour, sugar, horse feed and fowl feed, etc.

The following story was told to me by my mother many times over the years that I lived at Karekare.

On this particular day Dr Raynor had come down on the boat from Onehunga and was going back with the driver on the wagon that had all Mr Farley's heavy goods on board. The driver was Bill Stokes. When they got to the Karekare Point there was quite a bit of water still around it, so Stokes decided to wait awhile for the tide to drop a bit more.

Dr Raynor was in a hurry to get back to Piha and said, 'Come on what are you waiting for? Are you scared?'

That was enough for Bill Stokes; he put the horses into it and halfway round the wagon got overturned, losing all Mr Farley's goods. They had to cut the traces to get the horses out. Both got soaking wet and Dr Raynor had to foot the bills. (It pays to look before you leap if you don't want to pay for the leap.) Dr Raynor also brought donkeys to Piha in 1910 to pull the trucks of timber at the mill. After the mill closed down they turned them out in the valley and they roamed up the coast as far as Bethells.

The road that ran in front of my cottage.

Hans Peter Knutzen

Hans Peter Knutzen was born on 21 January 1863 at Falstead, Denmark. At an early age he went to sea and arrived in New Zealand waters in 1883 aboard the brigantine *Seagull*, which was to work on the New Zealand coast. He paid off at Dunedin and worked his way to Auckland, then in the northern gum fields. In 1895 he joined the Kauri Timber Company at Tairua and then began a career in the timber industry that was to last for 40 years. He came to Dr Raynor's Piha Mill in 1908 and in two years had taken over as manager, then spent two more with the Taupo Totara Timber Company where the full value of a large scale tramway operation could be observed, before he returned to Piha in 1912.

He now got the work started at Karekare Beach. It was necessary that the line run on trestles and in order to get maximum clearance from the sand, some of the trestles were to stand 16-feet high. While work progressed, bullocks struggled to keep the timber moving along to reach the local and Australian markets.

Danish-born Hans Knutzen, Piha Mill manager. Knutzen opened up the Piha valleys for new timber milling.

Timber milling on the West Coast   55

ABOVE Rising from the valley floor, the steep Piha tram section was breathtaking.

ABOVE RIGHT This image is used by historians and architects to demonstrate the perfect bach. Hans Knutzen enjoys a Sunday off work at Piha.

The New Zealand Government Railways were at this time buying large quantities of Piha timber and it was this interest that led them to line the entire operation in 1913 and purchase it outright in 1915, placing it under the control of the Stores Branch.

The annual cutting capacity of the Piha Mill was 4,000,000 super feet, but this figure was seldom achieved owing to the frequent interruption of operation by natural elements. The production from the mill between 1912 and when it closed down was about 14,000,000 super feet by the time the area had been completely cut out of all millable timber.

With the mill in full production and major transport problems overcome, Hans Knutzen searched for additional timber supplies. He obtained cutting rights for the Anawhata Valley north of Piha. Experience at Karekare had shown that moving the logs to the mill need present little problem if they constructed an additional tramway. The line was taken the length of Piha beach on trestles, to the hill separating it from Anawhata. From there it climbed up, following the course of Whites Creek then down the other side, with a hauler placed on top of the ridge.

It was fair weather railroading as the train ran weather and sand permitting. Southwesterly gales regularly whipped at the Tasman surf to beat the cliffs and tramway. Driven sand would pile high on the tramway, covering even the trestles that stood 16 feet or more above the beach. Some of the mill foreman's reports tell a clear story of the conditions.

July 1915	Heavy floods damaged tramline and trestles.
November 1915	Severe flooding damage, tramlines at Karekare, Pararaha and Whatipu. Permanent repairs not completed until January 1916.
March 1916	Heavy downpour of rain interfered with operation and damaged tramlines between Karekare and Whatipu.
May 1916	Serious floods in all creeks damaged tramlines, mill booms and Piha main driving dam, mill engine room flooded.
December 1916	Torrential rain washed out 26 sets of trestles, damaged bridges and altered course of the Whatipu creek.
February 1917	Torrential rain and heavy flooding again experienced, resulting in considerable damage to bridges and trestles.
July 1917	Gales and heavy rain, drifting sand again troublesome, an exceptionally wet winter.

With the mill finally closed down, all the equipment was sold to the King Country firms of Carter, Bennett and Punch of Ohakune. All the parts from the mill, after being dismantled, were taken over the tramway to Whatipu. Even the big mill boiler, weighing about 10 tons, went over the tramway balanced on the run down Skids Gully into Karekare by a giant kauri log. I can remember Bob Gibbons telling me all about it while having dinner with him at Whatipu in the winter of 1927. To take this tremendous weight, all the bridges were strengthened and it was still thought that the load would break loose and tear up the track, but all went well.

The kauri log also went down, balanced over the steep incline by a wagonload of old scrap that was not wanted. So to celebrate the end of the job the loopman sent it freewheeling back towards Piha. It shot over the edge at great speed, jumping the tracks and overturning into the bush. The men, with Hans Peter Knutzen still in charge, went down to the King Country.

New Zealand Railways inspectors tour the Anawhata Drop in 1910.

BELOW Tripping the Piha dam, 1912. It was said the roar could be heard in Auckland City.

BELOW LEFT The tramline crossing Piha Beach, with Lion Rock in the background.

Timber milling on the West Coast

The engines

As if the natural hazards were not enough, the operators faced yet another worry — tourists. The Karekare guest-house was flourishing and while it was a respectable and novel diversion for holiday makers to be photographed, parasols and all, seated on the logging bolster behind Sandfly, nightmare situations were created for loopmen on top of the hill by careless tourists who set out to walk up Skids Gully, totally ignorant of the danger from the descending load, let alone a runaway. It was a miracle that the line remained accident-free.

Sandfly was shipped to Onehunga and then to Newmarket workshops for overhauls and regauging, while work was completed on the Anawhata line. It was returned in company with A196, a small tank engine obtained from the maintenance branch for work on the Piha section.

A196 was built by Dale and Company of Scotland in 1873 and worked on the New Zealand Railway as A62 in Christchurch and Timaru until 1897, when it was transferred north to Wellington and worked as a shunter at Cross Creek. In 1905 it was loaned to the Maintenance Board for work at the Pencarrow Quarry and in 1906 was purchased by Maintenance for the job.

The Stores Branch took over ownership at Piha and, after being overhauled at the Newmarket workshop, A62 was delivered to Whatipu, partly dismantled, and taken over to Piha, where the old blacksmith completed the assembly. This engine then worked daily over the Piha–Anawhata section. For the duration of the job it was renumbered A196 and at Piha carried both numbers, one on each sidetank.

When the mill closed down A196 was again dismantled and transported back along the tramline to Whatipu and then to Newmarket for repairs and rebuilding before going under its own steam down to the Stores Branch tramway at Pakaka. It was finally written off on 31 March 1926 and displayed for a while at the Otahuhu workshops. Today it is in the care of a private museum.

A196 at Piha Mill. A kauri log is about to be jacked off the bolster into the storage yard.

The Pararaha Tunnel with Sandfly in front and Mt Zion in the background.

Right A flood near the tramline, 1922. The boy on the left of the two is me, aged eight.

Far right Snaking across the black sands of Piha, the government's NZ Rail 3"6 winds its way towards Lion Rock and the mill.

A196 with two big kauri logs crossing Piha Beach. Fuel for the hauler is being transported on the track at the rear.

Below, top Sandfly, with a loaded bolster of timber, takes on water from the creek before leaving for Whatipu. Winchelsea Guest House is in the background.

Below, bottom The Piha express, No. A196, towing logs to the Piha mill.

Right Knutzen and his Piha mill hands ungrate A62, which had a removable chimney, and get it ready for some serious work.

Charlie Cowan

Charlie Cowan was a typical New Zealand bushman, noted for his ingenuity and cheerful disposition in the face of difficulties. For a while he drove the Guthrie and Lanark engine from Karekare to Whatipu and later worked the hauler at the top of Skids Gully, Karekare. I was told he was driving this engine one day when a man was killed at Windy Point. This chap was working on the line and there was a south-west wind blowing at the time. Charlie blew the whistle before he got to Karekare Point, but with the wind blowing the sound away he did not hear it. When he saw the engine come round the corner he started to run along the wet sleepers, slipped and fell. Charlie had no hope of stopping the engine with all the trucks of timber behind. I was told that if he had only got over the side and hung on he would have had a better chance, but you can always be wise afterwards.

Early in 1918 my grandparents set off to America on a business trip and left Mr and Mrs Reg Eyre to look after the place while they were away. Mrs Eyre always seemed to have her blouse come out at the back and Charlie, being a bit of a prankster, kept saying, 'Get a big safety pin woman, that will fix it.' One night he came in for dinner and brought with him a big safety pin about 3 feet long and made from a bit of No. 8 fencing wire. 'Here you are,' he said, 'this should do it,' amidst roars of laughter from all at the table. I have seen this famous safety pin and it used to hang on the wall of the old dairy for years. I last saw it in the early thirties and don't know what happened to it but I have often wished that I had taken it off the wall and carefully kept it in memory of Charlie Cowan, being a bit of a prankster myself.

At the time there was an Englishman from Norfolk staying for a while and that night there was cold meat for dinner. On the way back from the hauler Charlie got some big huhus out of an old kauri log and quietly looking for a chance, slipped them under the meat before Mrs Eyre handed it to the chap. They all sat down and started to eat and a few seconds later one of them pushed its head out from under the meat. The Norfolk chap leapt up, his eyes as big as saucers. He was inclined to stammer and eventually spluttered, 'Good heavens woman you will have to have a look at that safe of yours.' He went on to say that he had been in the tropics, but had never seen anything so large before. Charlie of course got a fit of coughing and rushed outside to explain.

The art of pit-sawing

The pit-sawing of timber was a cheap method of utilising small stands of kauri trees in difficult places, for it was much easier to transport sawn timber than shifting a log weighing many tons through the thick bush down steep gullies.

Pit-sawyers worked in pairs with an oblong hole in the ground about 6 feet wide, the length depending on the length of the log to be sawn, and was deep enough for a man to stand upright over this pit. The log was rolled in and securely fastened to prevent any movement. Then, with one man on top of the log to guide the big saw and pull it up and another man underneath to pull it down, the process of cutting the log into slabs was commenced. It was hard to say which was the more difficult job, pulling the saw up and following the guideline (a string that enabled the man on top to keep the slab to the required thickness), or standing underneath and pulling the saw down, getting a shower of sawdust at the same time.

The men of this bygone age could cut boards and planks as even in thickness as a mechanised saw and many houses with weatherboards of pit-sawn timber are still standing today.

From round 1854 when timber mills were working at Kakamatua and Huia, till 1930 when the Waitakere Timber Company's mill at the head of the Anawhata closed down, about a score of mills had worked in the Waitakere Ranges.

Mr Bob Gordon told me of an old tunnel through a narrow ridge at Kakamatua. One log drive in this stream failed to lose its force by the time it reached the trams and the massive drive smashed its way through the outer walls and carried about 1000 logs out into the Huia Bay. So in an endeavour to prevent this and allow flood headwaters to calm, the tunnel was constructed.

Another mill was erected at the mouth of the Kakamatua in 1892. The machinery to operate the mill was from Karekare that had closed down in 1886. Mr Charles Murdoch from Karekare was again manager and came over to Huia to install and manage the mill for a while.

One of the early mills in the Kakamatua Stream was driven by water power and called the Niagara Saw Mill. When I saw the site in 1942, just past the concrete bridge work by the bridge at Huia Bay, only the old flat grassed area gave any indication of where the mill once was.

In 1928 I went with my father and Mr Con Grant right through the bush from the Nihotupu Dam to the Huia Dam, which was being built. The events I have described of pit-sawing are how I witnessed them. Even now, after all these years, I can see this big chap on top of the log who would have been well over 6 feet tall, go straight through that log about 30 feet long, without stopping. That was the first and last pit-sawing I had the honour to watch; previously all I knew had been told to me by early settlers and bushmen.

Shifting sands

By far the greatest problem, apart from floods, was drifting sand across the line at Karekare Beach, Pararaha and Whatipu. To cope with this, my mother said, gangs of men used horse scoops and shovels to try and keep it clear. When they saw the engines coming they would move the sand a few feet to the side and after it had gone out of sight sit down again. The first wind from that side brought it all back on the line again, so this seems like an early attempt on Parkinson's law, which means that work expands so as to fill the time available for its completion.

About this time the Manukau Bar changed its course so two lighthouses had to be built on top of Windy Point. The timber for them was all dragged up with horses; they had no sooner got them erected than the bar went back to its former course; they stand there today, still unused. That is the Manukau Bar though and I came to know its many moods in the 29 years I lived at Karekare.

Jack Sergeant

It was in the cab of the engine Sandfly that I had my first ride and I have treasured memories of the ride, this engine, and its capable driver, Jack Sergeant. Jack Sergeant began his railway career in Auckland in the pioneer days. He transferred later to the South Island and after driving the Invercargill Express for a while returned to Auckland to drive the Rotorua Express and then down the main trunk line before going to the Helensville Express, until his retirement.

Mander and Bradley's Mill, Nihotupu

On the West Coast Road from Waiatarua down to the Nihotupu Bridge (mainly scrub and second growth today) is the area where the finest kauri in the Ranges once thrived. The bush around the headwaters of the Nihotupu Stream was owned by John Hueston and Oliver Wasley, who had let the milling rights to Messrs Mander and Bradley. Frank Mander, who was known as 'Pop', was the senior partner in the firm and through his initiative and genius they overcame the problems that had prevented this area being worked earlier.

Situated in a valley about 1000 feet up, the main problem was to get the timber down in sufficient quantities so it could be carted to Auckland. So under Mr Mander's supervision, a tramway was built up to the top of the ridge and then down to the Henderson Valley via Dreamlands, as it is called now. In Maori, Rua te Whenua means 'the rumble of the earth'. It was said to have been given this name because when standing on top of the hill the roar of the surf on the coast seems to come to one's ears from out of the Nihotupu Valley. The tramway lowered the timber over 900 feet in about a mile. This was considered a real masterpiece in bush tramway construction then.

The fine stand of kauris was

At Whatipu in 1909, a group of mill hands show off the takings of a successful weekend hunting expedition.

milled in the late 1890s. To commemorate the visit to the mill at Nihotupu in 1896 of the Earl of Glasgow (who was then Governor of New Zealand), a giant kauri tree, 14 feet in diameter and 80 feet to the first branches, was named the Glasgow Tree. It was left standing but this now isolated giant of a tree rearing its head above the destruction of its former protective covering, got badly smoked in a bush fire and rather than waste the timber it was felled. Thus the last survivor of that magnificent stand of kauri bush in the area is gone forever. The mill was partly destroyed by fire in 1897 but was rebuilt and operated until the bush was worked out in 1899.

Jonny Toams

The timber mill days produced their share of characters and one of these, known of little today, was Jonny Toams, the woodcutter. For a time he was camping in Destruction Gully at the back of Whatipu and one day when Charlie Cowan was there with the engine, he saw Jonny and, always being on for a bit of fun, thought, 'This is it.' So he told him that Percey was not a bad sort of chap but if I was you I would keep a sharp eye on him round the full moon. Unknown to Jonny he told Percey the same thing and these two would go miles to avoid one another on a moonlight night. Of course everyone else was in the know and thought it a great joke. It was also Charlie who used to call Jonny 'Cemetery Tombs'.

Another time Jonny was carrying a sack of flour at the Whatipu wharf and there was a small hole in the bottom. This was a month's supply and someone saw it and yelled out, 'Hey Jonny, you're losing all your flour,' and back came the answer, 'All the better, be a damn sight easier to carry.'

I met Jonny in 1922 when he came to cut ti-tree for us. He pitched his tent up over the Clear Hill, as we called it then. The next day Wally Farley shot a wild boar and with my cousin Kathleen, we got the trotters and went and made pig tracks all round his tent. He came back from work, saw the tracks and must have thought, 'Hell, there is a big boar round here. I had better get out of it before dark.' So Jonny quickly rolled everything up in his mattress, tied it round with flax and bowled it all down the hill. I was in the paddock at the time and saw the bundle jumping the ti-tree bushes as it came down. It then landed on the road, jumping the fence into the paddock and scared about six month's growth out of a bunch of turkeys enjoying the late afternoon sun.

Another time Jonny came round from Whatipu to get stores and the Point was bad again. So Mrs Farley said he had better stay the night. They had only had the electric light going for a few weeks and Jonny had never seen it and knew even less about it. He was shown a room and told to turn it out before getting into bed, but Mr Laurie Farley thought he had better have a last look and see if Jonny was all right. Imagine his surprise to find Jonny standing on the bed trying to blow it out!

A few days after he had moved his camp down from over Clear Hill, Jonny told Wally Farley about the pig tracks round his tent. Wally was a bit like Charlie Cowan and myself and saw his chance to join in. So Wally told him Charlie was wise to move out because there was a large boar out by the The Companies (the gully below Lone Kauri farm), big as a Shetland pony and with his tail dragging on the ground. I think Jonny thought he had been very lucky to get out in time.

He was only a little chap but had a big appetite. He would have a dozen eggs for breakfast. For dinner he could eat a boiled snapper and a billy of potatoes. Talking of snapper, he used to go fishing at times and if he did not get a bite in about ten minutes, would cut the line up in little bits and throw it in. Next came the spare hook, sinkers and then the sugar bag. 'Oh, take the damn lot then,' he would say. About a month later he would come and buy a new line and start all over again. Well, that was Jonny.

Moffat Byles and Tommy Golter

Moffat Byles was an expert bushman and the Byles home was about 300 yards past Darkey's slab hut on the opposite side of the road. 'Darkey' was Martin Sanders (pronounced Saunders), he was one of the best-known characters of the ranges.

I first met 'Moff' in 1922 and again in later years when he came through Karekare on his way to Pararaha after kauri gum. On one of these trips he had a Maori with him and they both had horses. The Maori found it a bit lonely and weird at night in the gorge, so he got up one morning and cleared out, cutting Moff's horse loose so he could not follow him. Moff arrived on foot about two hours behind the horse and told me what had taken place. I said that I had heard his horse go over the middle bridge in front of the mill just after daylight. He talked for a while and then said, 'Well I will have to beat it,' and was off at a trot for Henderson.

About a week after the Maori had cleared out Moff was back again with another mate. This time a Pakeha and they set off for the Pararaha Gorge again. A few days later this chap came in one night to get more stores and had some strange tales to tell us. He said he could not get to sleep the first night as Moff just sat on the end of his bed sharpening a sheath knife and feeling the edge.

The Lone Kauri as it was when Moff and Tommy Golter gave the climbing display in 1912.

The Pararaha Gorge. Moff's camp was just round the first bend on the right where there is a grassy slope studded with outcrops of rock. The same spot was chosen by Fred Gibbons when he built a kauri-paling shack there in 1930.

Another thing that startled him was to see Moff mount a lancewood stick and canter down to the creek with a billy in one hand to get water. On the way back, as though riding a flighty horse, he would see something on the bank and shy at it, going sideways round it and then bolting into the ti-tree and spilling all the water. This of course made breakfast late.

Riding a lancewood is one thing and climbing a kauri was another. Moff was an expert at this and could climb a kauri that was already 50 feet high when William the Conqueror landed in Britain, with no more trouble than an urban dweller has at sitting down to the table.

My mother told me how he and a half-caste Maori named Tommy Golter, gave an exhibition of kauri climbing on the Lone Kauri for members of the

With his brother Ru they could put up a nikau whare just like the old time Maoris. Not a drop of water would come in. They built the whare for Cameron Johnson, the painter, at Cutting Creek, and my mother often told me what a splendid job it was. Another kind of whare they used to put up in no time was made from kauri palings. These were split from a piece of kauri with a paling knife and were about 3 feet long and 4–5 inches wide. This method was used quite often in those days and would certainly cut down on building costs today.

When I first went to Karekare all the valley was fenced in kauri palings. Two wires were twisted round the top and two round the bottom and each post had a hole through the top to take a piece of kauri 6 inches wide that ran from post to post. It was like this up till 1928.

Timber milling on the West Coast

Waitemata Council in 1912. She saw the display and said after they got up in the branches they took their boots off and jumped from branch to branch with a short axe in their hands, which they drove into the branch as they landed to steady themselves. It was a tremendous feat and I only wish I could have seen it.

Moff retired in Henderson and I last heard of him in 1952 and like the great kauri forests, he had all but faded away.

Where the kauri flourished the tree was climbed and a process known as 'bleeding' was carried out. To climb the tree special equipment was used; this consisted of a pair of boots that had a specially made spikes about 2 inches long protruding from each toe, and for the hands a pair of climbing irons that looked like hooks, steel implements about 12 inches long and sharpened like picks. Then a wooden seat attached to a rope, anything up to about 200 feet long, as well as a bag for the gum, and an axe. By alternately reaching for a higher hold with his climbing irons and spiked boots, he was able to go vertically up the trunk just about as fast as he could walk along the ground. After he had reached the forks, he would drop the rope over one side of a branch and sit in the seat on the other side. Then by controlling the end of the rope that was hanging, he was able to lower or check his descent to the ground as he wished.

The process of bleeding was carried out at intervals about 18 inches apart. The tree climber made cuts or what were called 'taps' in the bark around the trunk. The taps were usually arrow-shaped and cut deeper into the bark near the apex where it almost reached the sap. Then about six feet or so further down the process was repeated and so on down the trunk. After six or eight months the tree was visited again and the gum that had accumulated in the taps was carefully chipped out. This, the lifeblood of the kauri, was called bash-bled gum and although it did not bring as much as other types it was well worth collecting and Moff spent quite a bit of his time 'upstairs and downstairs'. Many settlers were engaged in this bleeding process or otherwise searching in the boo-cow or rubbish at the foot of the tree for the gum that had over the centuries fallen to the ground.

Boo-cow Tom

What I am about to relate was told to me by my mother, grandmother and Mr Bob Gordon of Huia. I later heard it from Mr Bob Gibbons himself, who was mill manager at the time.

One day in the winter of 1927, I had gone round to Whatipu with my father to get supplies that came down by the boat from Onehunga. It was

The amazing kauri steeplejacks gathering gum in the topmost branches of the trees.

The name Henderson comes from Thomas Henderson who had gangs of pit sawyers working for him round the district. In 1846 he established a mill at the head of the tidal waters of the Henderson Creek where the logs were taken to be milled. He purchased the whole of Henderson Valley right up to the top of the ridge and the timber from this area kept the mill operating until about 1860.

not due till the afternoon so we took the horses up to the Gibbons' and they gave us lunch. While we had lunch the story was told again and you would really have to see the situation to believe it.

Boo-cow was known to all the bush workers in the Ranges at the time; it is the leaves and rubbish found around the base of kauri trees and was used to seal leaks in the big timber dams holding the water to drive the logs downstream to the farms or hauling out sites. The correct method they used in stopping the leaks was to walk along a plank at the top of the dam and sprinkle the rubbish into the water so it would be drawn into the cracks and stop the leaks.

A new chap to come to the Waitakere Ranges was nicknamed Boo-cow Tom because of the following incident. Tom had stated that he was an experienced bushman so he was told to boo-cow the dam one morning. But not knowing what to do he asked the cook who said it meant stopping the leaks in the dam with leaves. So off went Tom to do the job, but as he had not returned at midday, Bob Gibbons who was mill manager, thought he had better go and see what had happened to him. As he came in sight of the dam he was stunned to see Tom on the downstream side of the dam poking nikau leaves and other leaves into the cracks with his knife, but naturally the big force of the water kept pushing them out. This was enough to make any bushman's hair stand on end but what made Bob Gibbons gasp was the sight of Tom stepping all around and over the trip mechanism, a very delicately set apparatus for holding in place the gate of the dam. All it needed was a pull or kick on the wire running away from it to release the large force of water and logs. Bob Gibbons told me he spent some very anxious moments before he got to telling Tom how close to death he had been. It was this stunt that earned him the name Boo-cow Tom.

A natural dam of kauri-heads, which had been left over from the mill days. They became jammed together in the Pararaha Gorge after the big flood on the night of 24 December 1927.

The Karekare Waterfall in flood. This would have looked like a drop from a tap if Tom had accidentally tripped the dam; a million gallons or more plus the logs would have carried him who knows where.

Martin (Darkey) and Agnes Sanders

Martin Sanders was one of the best known and colourful characters of the Waitakere Ranges. He was a native of Jamaica, as black as the ace of spades and his proud boast was that he was the first 'white man' to cross the Waitakere Ranges. He was known to all as Darkey, but he did not like this name and if it was used in front of him would say, 'Look mister, not so much of this 'Darkey' from you. It's Mr Martin Sanders and don't you forget it.'

He was living at Muriwai for a while and was brought over to the West Coast Road by Pa Bethell. A kauri paling hut was erected for him by Moff and Ru Byles at the foot of what was to become known as Darkey's Hill.

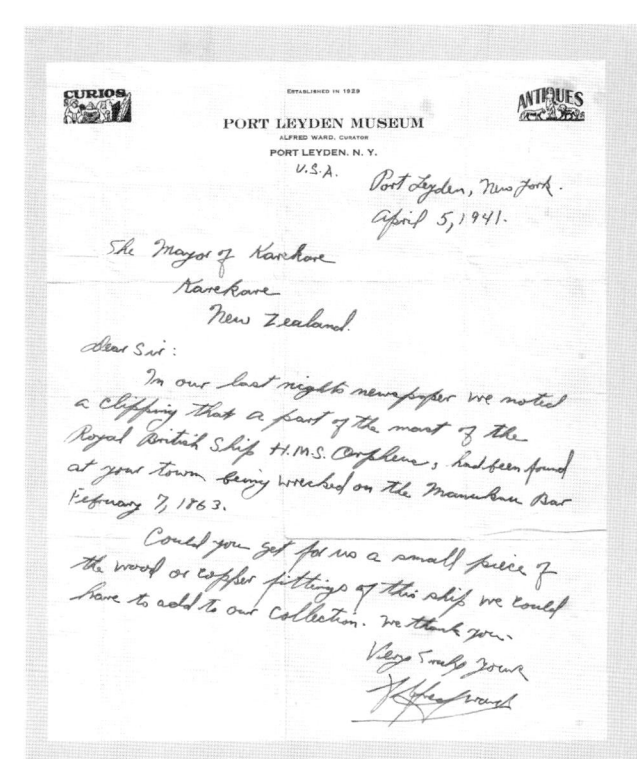

Shipwrecks

HMS *Orpheus*, at 1706 tons, was practically a new vessel at the time she was wrecked on the Manukau Bar on 7 February 1863. In addition to sails, she had a steam engine capable of driving her at about 12 knots and it was under the command of Commodore W.T. Burnett, C.B. She was attempting to enter the Manukau when she struck the edge of the north bank in the early afternoon. It seems that Commodore Burnett mistook the Pararaha headland for Paratutui and turned in too soon. I was told that one man informed the captain, before she struck, that he was off course and for daring to tell the captain he was wrong was placed in irons.

About 2 p.m. the cutter, with all the records and valuable papers, was sent ashore and they reached the beach near Cutter Rock as it has been known ever since. Some say that it carried bullion, which is thought to be still buried in the sand near the rock. The men were all paid in gold sovereigns then and if the cutter was overturned in the breakers getting in they could be well down in the sand now.

At about 7 o'clock that night, on 7 February 1863, the position of the men on board was critical and when the masts began to go overboard it was seen that nothing could save the men. The terrific pounding of the breakers, which continually swept over her, was taking its toll, so that at dawn all that remained of this proud man-of-war was the stump of a mast showing above the water.

Of the 259 officers and men on board, 189 were drowned, this being the largest number of lives lost in any shipping disaster on the New Zealand coast. The bodies were washed ashore all along the coast and it was impossible to take them all to recognised cemeteries, so many were buried on the hill-sides and sand-hills along the west coast and some in the Manukau shoreline.

Between 1820 and 1940 all the crews of other boats wrecked at the entrance to the Manukau and along the coastline perished. The barque *Helena* of 265 tons was wrecked at Bethells Beach on 20 September, 1853. Captain Brown and his crew battled a westerly gale for many days, which slowly drove them towards the land and after failing to cross the Manukau Bar was headed for the beach at Bethells. Captain Brown was among those who drowned. Only four of the crew survived.

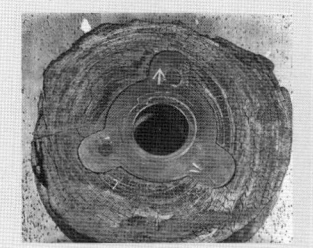

Of the ships that were wrecked at the southern end of Muriwai Beach, the best remembered are the barquentine *May* (237 tons, oak construction, all crew drowned except champion swimmer Watti Dunn) and the barques *Concordia* in 1902 (timber load, Russian crew, one life lost) and *Kinclare* in 1904 (741 tons, ironclad, total wreck on beach, no loss of life).

A letter my father received from the Port Leyden Museum in New York, USA, asking if we could get a piece of wood or a copper fitting for their collection.

The pully from the base of the centremast of the HMS *Orpheus*, which I found still attached to the centre section. It was found on a sand-hill between Mt Zion and Pararaha, uncovered during a south westerly storm in February. The government arrow can be seen on the brass. After the photo was taken my father presented the centremast to a museum.

His chief occupations were gum-digging and cutting firewood. Once a month he would go into town and sell gum. Then get drunk and quite often arrested and taken before court where he would be fined or sent to jail and was always put to work in the laundry, 'a job that was always kept open for him,' he would say. I remember how he used to tell Wally Farley (Mr Willy he always called him), 'If ever you get sent to jail, be sure and dodge the crusher (rock pile), it is easier carrying the laundry baskets for the ladies.' I think this was how he met Agnes, his wife, who was an Irishwoman.

On one occasion when he had been put in the lock-up for the night, he kept calling out that Agnes was alone in town, then started to call her. You can imagine his surprise when she answered him from another cell, for she had also been arrested.

They always left the horse at Waikumete and then got the train to town. After getting off the train on the return journey, Darkey often put Agnes on the horse, tied her feet together under the horse's stomach to prevent her falling off and, with him holding the reins, they would start off for home.

The Irish in Agnes at times caused her to turn her wrath on those who annoyed her, but people liked her and would tell of the spotless condition of the shack and the tabletop always scrubbed white. Those who had afternoon tea at her place said it was an experience you would never forget for she had everything laid out neatly with fancy cloths and doilies, just as though she was serving guests at a hotel, but this is understandable as before she married Darkey she was a waitress at the mansion, the home of Sir George Grey on Kawau Island.

Agnes died before Darkey. She died at the shack on Darkey's Hill while he was serving one of his jail sentences. The coroner established that she had died from natural causes. Darkey, who had been released from jail, then buried her on the hill above the shack, wrapped in a blanket, and he erected a picket fence around the grave. It was her wish that she should be buried on the hill and Darkey told Wally Farley she said that's because she knew he would have to carry her up there.

Agnes Sanders at the cottage she and Darkey lived in.

On one of his trips to town after Agnes died, and while drunk, Darkey fell down a lift well and lost the sight in one eye. Sometime later Wally Farley was going by his place with the mail and Darkey came out to get it and told him all about what had happened. He had a patch over one eye and being black as the ace of spades with a white patch on his face was enough to make any good horse not want to go any closer. After Wally had managed to quieten the horse he said, 'Oh, I wouldn't worry Martin, get a glass eye.' Darkey replied, 'I don't think that would be any good Mr Willy because the chap in the next bed in the hospital told me he had one and he couldn't even see to read the paper with it.'

Darkey once told Constable Douglas of Henderson that when his father died his mother later married a Scotsman, so he became a Scotsman automatically. Ever after that Constable Douglas called him the Automatic Scotsman. Just to prove that he wasn't really a Scotsman I will give the show away by letting on that his mother was a native of Jamaica and his father a native from West Africa.

These periodical drinking bouts by Darkey and many of the bush workers were their only form of entertainment after months of isolation in the kauri bush camp and gum fields. I often wonder how today's generation would react if they had the same conditions to live and work in and got the same pittance of half a century ago.

I first met Darkey in 1922 and his old shack was starting to tumble down, then finally collapsed. He still continued to live under the gable roof which had come to rest on the ground. I last saw him a few weeks before Christmas of 1923 when I was going to Waikumete with Wally Farley and his boy Woee (his sisters' short form of Wallace). When he got to Darkey's place he noticed that his stores left in the box on the roadside from a previous trip had not been collected, so went in to see if he was ill. We found him in bed and too weak to get up, so Wally went in under the collapsed roof while Woee and I peeped in from the side. He saw us and called out, 'Merry Christmas boys'. I will always remember these last words. We had brought all his things in and left him as comfortable as possible while we went on to Waikumete where Wally informed Constable Douglas of the Henderson Police station, who came out and took him into the city. He did not return to the collapsed shack and died later in 1924.

So farewell to Darkey and Agnes. He was kind to her and would always share any of his surplus money. Storekeepers also found him very honest and could depend on him paying his account.

PUBLISHER'S NOTE Events from this page forward have been given a chronological order for ease of reading; the entries do not strictly follow the order Wally wrote them in.

1914

I was born in Auckland on 11 December 1914. The first home my parents had was in Ethel Street, Mt Albert. My father was then with the Tramway Co. and after a few weeks they moved to Warnock Street, Grey Lynn.

I was taken out to Karekare for the first time in February 1915 as my parents wished to have me christened there. I was christened on 7 February 1915, 52 years to the day after the sinking of HMS *Orpheus* on the Manukau Bar.

My earliest memory of Karekare is about the middle of 1918 and the two things that are so clear from that visit are being given a ride in the engine, Sandfly, by driver Jack Sergeant, and going up the Scotsman, as it was called, with Elfreda Eyre, to catch her black mare Judy. She was 12 then and lived only another nine years, after a short illness she died in 1927. Even now, after all those years, I can see myself carrying the bridle and climbing up the hill, under the pohutukawa trees above the house, after her. We caught the horse round by the 'Orchard Bush', as it was called. She lifted me on for a ride back while she held the bridle. I have no photo of the event so you will have to imagine, you can see the little boy of 3 ½ carrying the bridle up the hill and then riding back while she held the bridle and with the other hand was ready to catch me should I fall. I did not fall, so even then was following in my mother's footsteps by becoming a good rider.

Me as a youngster. Taken at the Grey Lynn home, 1915.

I can only remember a little about the Grey Lynn home, but one thing has stuck in my memory over the years was going out one day with my parents and getting in among a lot of turnstiles. We had quite a job to get out. I often spoke of it to my mother who said she could not remember about it. Over 50 years later I told a friend about it and she said she thought it would be the old zoo.

Another thing I have always remembered is going out one day with my mother to visit one of her friends and have afternoon tea with her in the tram. I got on a new pair of patent leather shoes, which I was very proud of. When the tram came along everyone wanted to get on first. Well, the crux of it all is that a man trod on my shoe and made a big scratch on it. It completely ruined my day and spoilt the afternoon tea as well, for I could not eat any biscuits the kind lady gave me, but kept looking at my shoe and wondering why the world is cursed with clumsy people.

Next door to us at Grey Lynn were Mr and Mrs Charlie Bailey. He was a famous New Zealand boatbuilder and built many fine boats over the years, in fact the art is still carried on under his name today, that of Charles Bailey and Sons Ltd, Beaumont Street.

Gwenith Bailey and I were good playmates as we got older until her parents left to go and live on Norfolk Island about the middle of 1916. I did not see her again until I was returning from the war and Guadalcanal on 5 January 1945 and spent the night there.

After they had gone we lived on at Grey Lynn for another three years and I was taken out to Karekare again on some occasions, but do not remember anything of these visits. At three years old I can remember quite well watching at the gate for my father to come home from work at the Tram Barn.

The Hereford bull outside the stockyard is one of the three I purchased at Tuakau on 10 October 1938. His name was Mangutia Forester. Sticking out of the shed is the rear of the 1926 Hudson truck I used to drive up the bulldozed roads for firewood.

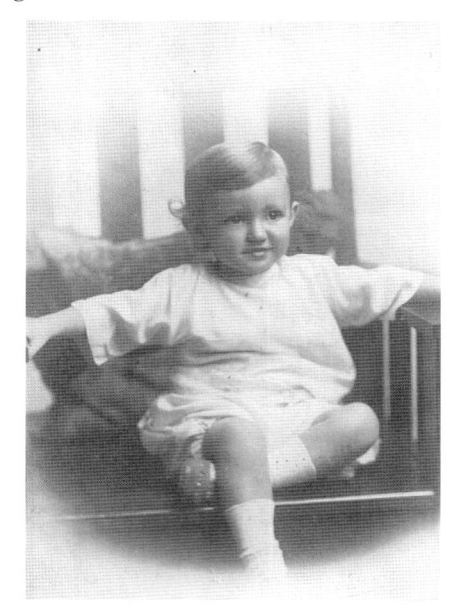

My third birthday, the 11th of December, 1917.

1919

Stanmore Bay, Whangaparaoa

In April 1919 my parents, along with my mother's sister Madge and her husband, my uncle George, decided to buy a farm at Stanmore Bay. I think it was about 44 acres and took in all the foreshore so we had our own private beach. My memory is so good that I can even remember the name of the man they bought it from; he was Mr Lappin, a big chap and rather fond of practical jokes as you will see.

The first night at the farm the men were all down in the cowshed talking after Lappin had shown them around the place. It gradually got dark and my father and uncle were talking by themselves for a few minutes. Lappin, who had moved into the shadows, came up behind my uncle and let out a roar like a bull. George jumped about six feet in the air and no doubt thought, 'This is the end of the road.' When they got back to the house we all had a good laugh, except my uncle, who took a while to get over it. I remember how I kept laughing and thought it was very funny, my mother kept saying, 'You should not laugh like that, suppose it had been you.'

The next day we got in the boat and went out for a row around the bay. As we came in, my father put the oars down and stood up in the bow to do something with the anchor. The boat then got broadside on and the next thing everyone was shot out into about three feet of water. It gave me quite a fright as I was only 4 $1/2$. My mother grabbed me and pulled me away from the boat, which was nearly on top of us, upside down. She called out that we were all right so he dragged the boat away and into shore where he righted it. Sopping wet we made for the house and that was my first lesson with boats: look where you are going or end up where you are not looking.

In those days a road ran from Arkles Bay to the end of Stanmore Bay beach. This was the only road, all clay and a bog in the winter. After getting off the boat at Arkles Bay you had to go by horse and sledge along the road down to the beach, then along the beach to the house. Each morning after milking, the cream cans had to be taken on the sledge along the beach and over the hill to the wharf at Arkles Bay. With no roads the only way of getting to Whangaparaoa Peninsula or any of the bays before then was by boat and the service was run by the *Orewa* from Auckland.

I can remember several trips down to Auckland and back after we had settled in on the farm. The one I think most noteworthy was when my mother and myself, along with Aunt Madge and her boy Keith, were returning to Arkles Bay from Auckland on the *Orewa*. The wind was from the north-east as we steamed out of Auckland and I did not know then, but am a firm believer now, in what the Irishman said that the north-east wind is no good to anyone, it doesn't matter which direction it is coming from. After leaving the harbour and turning north we were head on into it, pitching and rolling, which had most of the passengers struggling to get to their cabins as hanging over the edge was too dangerous. I can even now, after all these years, see my aunt being thrown from one side of the cabin to the other and looking as green as the sea.

When it came to dinner time my mother made a brave attempt to take me up to the dining saloon where there were only four others all trying to look as though they had been round Cape Horn in a windjammer and this wasn't much at all. My mother soon left as she could not eat anything and left me in the care of a steward. I was not troubled with the action of the ship and was enjoying my dinner, much to the amazement of the steward who kept saying, 'My word sonny, I will have to tell the Captain about this.' One by one they left and I was alone in the saloon with him. I finished the first course and then said I would have plum pudding for sweets and still feeling fine and all the time being watched by him, then asked if I could have some more. He nearly collapsed; I can see it all so clearly now after all these years and just as if it happened yesterday. Having finished dinner, which I did enjoy, the steward took me back to my mother in the cabins and I sat down on the bunk and hung onto the side as the rolling got worse. The good ship *Orewa* was now head-on to it and had just left Browns Bay where some of the passengers had managed to get ashore, leaving their paper bags behind them.

After what seemed ages to all and to my Aunt Madge, who was not able to get out of that bunk, the steward put his head in the door and said Arkles Bay was in sight. As we came alongside the wharf, the captain came off the bridge to apologise for the rough trip and said it was the worst he had known and that some of the seats had been washed off the back. I will always remember that trip and how my aunt, while riding on the sledge over the hill from Arkles Bay, kept saying, 'I will never go on the boat again.' It was tough talk for there was no other way of getting there then.

At 4 1/2 I was ready to start work on the farm and had to learn to ride a horse as well. Each day, regardless of the weather, I went down to the paddocks with the dog and brought 30 cows up to the shed, and later I helped to feed about 15 calves, then wash and dry the separator. I can remember so well the little blue coat that I had and how my mother used to put it on for me and then watch from the veranda which looked towards the paddocks on one side and the beach on the other, as I set off.

After the morning milking was over and breakfast finished, my father set off with the cream cans on a sledge for Arkles Bay. I then went with my mother to catch the blue mare called Jessie. I remember being lifted on by my mother and we would go down to the beach for the riding lesson, but first go with my father as far as the end of the beach. I was quick to learn and soon could stay on at a canter, but there were a few spills, which you will have to have before you make a good rider.

We used to grow quite a lot of maize for the cows. My father and my uncle, ploughing and sowing it. As soon as it was ready they would cut it and I would carry it in bundles with my mother and aunt and feed it to the cows. This was the only kindergarten I ever knew, but it just seemed to be born in me my mother said in later years, that this work must be done if the farm was to be a success. I used to listen to the conversation, unknown to them, and even at the age of five soon knew that they were dependant on the monthly cream cheque. So I would quietly toil away long before I went to school as I liked the place with our own private beach and wanted to help get it paid off.

On the East Coast Bay is Tindalls Beach. It was then Tindalls farm and I often went over with my father to see him on farm business.

Another neighbour was Bill Craddock, a real toiler too, who like old Joe at Karekare, did not believe manual labour was a Spaniard. He would dig up an acre of ground in a day with a spade and my father would talk a lot about him in the evening. There was one spot of trouble though, his wife was an RC [Roman Catholic] and they did not get on so everything that went wrong was an RC so and so.

On the peninsula in those days just about everybody had a farm except the storekeeper and school teacher. Other neighbours were Polkinghornes, who owned all the dairy flats next to our farm, and the other families, the Kirkcaldys and Drummonds further up the hill. I often went with my father across Polkinghornes' flats as he always called them, to see Mr Polkinghorne and discuss farming techniques.

Kirkcaldy's farm was up on the hill at the back of us and my father and uncle had to go up each day and also milk their cows after ours were finished. I do not know why they had to do this as I was a bit young to remember all the details, but think they could have had an illness up there. I can remember though things getting rowdy at times and my uncle was not doing his share of work. Things drifted on for a few months and then it was decided to sell the farm and my uncle and aunt left about October in 1920; we were to remain on till the farm was sold.

I can't remember the exact location of the Drummond farm but it must have been not far up the hill as I started school with Muriel Drummond in February 1921. She often came home with me along the beach and we all went for a swim as the water was only a few yards from the house. After a bite to eat she would come with me to bring the cows up and was just as good at it as I was. I think she was the eldest in her family and according to tradition the eldest one was expected to cope with anything, including the impossible. After the farm was sold and we left to return to Karekare I did not see her again and have often wondered what happened to her. Whangaparaoa Road joined the metal road from Arkles Bay. It was just before the junction where the school was situated.

My brother Dudley, turned three on 16 January 1920, and on 6 March 1920 my other brother John, was born. I can remember now after all this time the day Mum came home with him. My father, with us two boys, had taken the sledge over to Arkles Bay to meet the boat and as I have said before that was the only means of transport then. It is strange how some pictures in my mind are so clear while others I have to think hard to get them down as I want them. The point I am getting at is I have a picture in my mind of seeing the boat come into the wharf at Arkles Bay, I can clearly see Mum sitting on the sledge which had a seat on it and nursing John, with us walking beside it as we came along Stanmore Bay beach. It was a pleasure meeting her on the wharf with the baby.

In late May with my father and uncle and his boy Keith, I would go over the hill and across to the Wade River. The farmer was going to swim his cows over to the other side for winter grazing, on the low tide. This he did every year and we were to give a hand to get them started into the river. They had all been across before except one; she did not want to go so a rope was put over her horns and two men got into a boat with the idea of making her swim behind. As the rope came tight and she could not free herself she evidently thought what is the good of a boat if you can't use it, so took a mighty leap in to it (just what I thought was going to happen). The real joke was that one of the men in the boat could not swim and while he was being rescued the cow came back to the bank and got out. Everyone was now back on the same side, minus the boat which had sunk, so it had to be called a day.

1920

The event I am about to describe took place I think about August in 1920. We were just finishing breakfast when there was a loud noise the likes of which I had never heard before and it seemed to be up in the sky. This was indeed strange, whatever could it be, so we all rushed outside and looked up in the air and to my amazement there was a seaplane circling round the bay. I knew that such things existed having been told there was a flying school at Kohimarama where pilots were training for World War I.

The plane landed on the water and taxied up to our beach. There was a mad rush along the beach and I have never run so fast as I tried to get there first. I just stood beside it and gazed in amazement as the pilot and two passengers got out on to the float and then stepped onto the beach. Of all the pictures in my mind, none is clearer than this one and I could point to just about the exact spot on the beach where it came in. I would have been more stunned though if I had known then that just 11 years later I was to become a pilot myself.

I know that the pilot was the famous World War I airman, Captain George B. Bolt, and it was a Boeing seaplane from Walsh Brothers flying school at Kohimarama. After about half-an-hour on the beach it taxied out in to the bay and took off for the return flight; I am sure I am one of the few living who can remember the event.

I was to get to know Captain Bolt very well during my Aero Club days in the thirties when he held all three positions of ground engineer, commercial pilot and advanced flying instructor to the Wellington Aero Club. He also flew the first airmail run from Auckland to Dargaville in the same plane not long after the Stanmore Bay flight. Before he retired he was ground engineer for TEAL and then Air New Zealand. George Bolt Memorial Drive is named in his honour. Of all the thousands who go over this drive, I wonder how many know what it means or the history of this man?

The next big event was me getting my brother John to start walking at

My brother, Dudley Badham.

nine months in November 1920. I can see my mother at the stove getting the dinner ready and my two brothers playing on the floor. After a while I stood John up by a chair and then held out my arms and said, 'Come on.' He took a few shaky steps and I caught him and he then wanted to keep on doing it. I then said, 'Look Mum, I have got John walking,' so she turned around, had a look and was quite excited. 'Quick,' she said, 'run down to the cowshed and tell your father to come and have a look,' so off I went like a shot. He came back with me and could not believe his eyes as John kept going back and forth with no idea of stopping this side of Christmas. After a few moments Dad had to return to the cowshed to finish the milking and somehow we got through the dinner with John raring to get out of his highchair and have a final go before it got dark, and Dudley wanting to see him do it again. At one point, I said 'Should we let him take the cows back to the paddock?' but thought he might go this way and the cows that way or fall by the way.

At Christmas 1920 I had grave apprehension about the ability of Santa to get his reindeer on the *Orewa*, so Muriel Drummond agreed with me that there was no point in putting the ladder up against the chimney. I think we got a little hat each through the post to keep the sun out of our eyes in the summer and the rain in the winter.

Another event that has come to mind was just before my uncle and aunt left was that Dudley and their second boy Ron used to get their father's hobnailed boots, put them on and go down to the beach and make tracks with what they called 'watertight feet mark boots'.

In February 1921 I was to go to school as well as get the cows and feed

The Flying School

The Flying School was operated by the Walsh brothers and Ruben Dexter, on the foreshore at Mission Bay. During the eight years of its operation from 1915 to 1923, the school trained 107 pilots, who were granted aviators certificates by the Royal Aero Club of England. In November 1915 the school was officially appointed by the Government to train New Zealanders for the Royal Flying Corps; only the sons of the wealthy could afford the £125 training fee.

The first seaplane the school owned was the 'Walsh Flying Boat', powered by an Anzoni 80hp radial engine, which the Walsh brothers, Leo and Vivian, had designed and built under their house. This plane was the first flying boat designed and built in the Southern Hemisphere. It made its maiden flight in the Waitemata Harbour on New Year's day 1915, piloted by Vivian Walsh. The school also operated a Caudorn Type F seaplane powered by a Le Rhone 66 70 hp rotary engine. The British Government had given the school a number of DH-9 land planes, but these were never used as the Walsh brothers considered American seaplanes more reliable and easy to handle.

These seaplanes included two B and W seaplanes powered by a single six-cylinder water-cooled Hall-Scott A5 engine of 125 hp giving them a top speed of 75 mph. They first flew in June 1916 and were the first aircraft built by the new giant Boeing Aircraft Company. The New Zealand flying school purchased these planes from William Boeing, who started the company, and they arrived in Auckland on 12 October 1918.

After the World War I ended on 11 November 1918, the school turned to charter flights and joyrides to remain solvent and on 16 December 1919 flew the first airmail in New Zealand from Auckland to Dargaville. This was my father's 32nd birthday and we were on the farm at Stanmore Bay that day.

The New Zealand Government took over the assets of the flying school from 1 September 1924 for £10,000.

A World War I Avro 504K, Karekare Beach in February 1932. The pilot was Captain Brake. The aircraft had three cockpits; the pilot sat in front one. It had a 110 hp rotary Lr Rohn engine and was fitted with a flip switch.

out maize. As my uncle and aunt had left about October I had to help more than ever with my father doing all the milking on his own. Each morning when he left with the cream cans on the sledge, I would go with him to school. Muriel and I would then walk home together, sometimes her mother or my mother would come along to meet us.

It was about mid-April that the farm was sold and preparations were made to leave. My father had thought of going to another farm at Whangamata, but my mother's father, Mr Farley, was not in the best of health and wanted us to come back to Karekare. I was sorry to leave in one way as the bay was a lovely place. From the morning we left till I next saw it was exactly 52 years, on 20 March 1973. I was with a friend and two of her cousins from England and they took a photo with their movie camera of the old home, which would often be shown in the evenings to all their friends in England. I don't think my parents would have thought it possible to go straight to it after all these years and all the farm covered with houses. Only the old home remains and it is still the best spot on the beach.

Back to Karekare

I cannot remember anything of the day we left, the trip on the boat to Auckland, or our stay overnight in the city. This is strange when all the other events from the time we arrive at the end of 1920 are so clear. The part I can remember is the next morning when my mother, with us three boys, went down to the railway station to get the train for Waikumete, while my father went out to Onehunga with the furniture. It had to be taken out with a wagon and horses and then manhandled onto the launch, *Outlaw*, for the trip down to Whatipu and then horses again along the beach to Karekare.

I can see us now getting off the train at Waikumete and meeting my uncle Wally Farley, with the coach and horses, who had left at 5 a.m. that morning. At 12 o'clock we got into the coach and started the long five-hour drive to the coast, the horses having had a two-hour spell that they always got at Waiatarua. I can not remember

The home that we came to in 1921. The room at the end with the window was my father and mother's room, the one in the middle with the bunks was for myself and my two brothers. There is a sitting room at the other end, which later became my sister's room.

much of that five-hour drive, but can see my grandmother pushing the gate by the woodbox and coming out to meet us as the coach stopped. So, back to Karekare again. I had not seen Karekare since 1919 and it was to be my home for the next 29 years.

Once again it was my job to get the cows and this time they were not in paddocks but had 500 acres to roam over. This called for a new kind of skill, the art of tracking to see which way they had gone. I was to become quite good at it over the years and could soon tell about how old a track was and what colour the animal was that I was tracking. This knowledge was greatly improved on and put to good use on the many wild pig hunting trips that took place after our arrival. In the following years up till 1930 we practically lived on wild pork in the winter and there is nothing better for meat as they lived on fern roots. I have a perfect pair of wild boar tusks given to me by my mother from a hunting trip she was on with Wally Farley in 1904. He told her to stand in a flax bush so he would know where she was if he got a chance to shoot.

On the hunting trips it was my job to carry the gun home if we got any pigs. This was a long barrel 303 Lee Enfield from World War I and no light weight for a boy of eight to carry through the bush.

The old bush tramline was still there and you could get on it by the house and walk right down the beach as late as December 1927. There was a big flood then that damaged it badly in front of the house and where it crossed the creek on its journey to the beach and on to the South Rock.

There was now the luxury of electricity. We did not have it at Stanmore Bay. I was taken down to the powerhouse and shown how the water came

The view from Warclates Bend at the top of the Karekare Cutting. From the road there is a drop of 800 feet in a mile and a half. The horses could smell home and did not want to stop and admire the view.

Winchelsea House, 1930. Behind the house are the stables, glasshouse, what was my room in the late 1920s, then the calf house, calf paddock, fowl house and duck run. Just behind the chimney of the house is the sitting room, added on by Mr Charlie Hyde in 1928.

The Karekare Point with one of the 9x9 sleepers still bolted to the rocks, 1936.

On the Karekare Road this side line ran from the mill at the bottom of The Cutting by the bridge. This is where today's baches are situated.

down the big 6-inch jarrah pipe and on to the pelten wheel that started turning with a roar like thunder. A 4-inch wide belt on to a pulley behind, turning a shaft with another pulley at the other end, drove the generator, which was 110 volts. The water came along a wooden flume from the top of the waterfall into a 600 gallon tank and down the 6-inch jarrah pipe with a drop of 180 feet to the powerhouse below. This gave a pressure of 80 pounds to the square inch and with a full head of water developed, about 15 horsepower. At this time the pelten wheel was what they called undershot, meaning that the water from the nozzle was directed into the cups on the bottom of the wheel. Just before Christmas 1932 we changed this procedure to overshot as we reckoned on getting more power with the cups full of water as they went over. This theory proved to be correct and the timber for the new pelten wheel bed was 9x9 kauri sleepers from Karekare Point that had been there since 1918 when the mill closed down. They were as sound as the day they were bolted to the rocks and, after all these years, with saltwater dashing over them, would ring like a bell if hit with the back of an axe. It was a big job getting them off as each bolt had to be cut through with a hacksaw using up a lot of blades and many hours of work. They had been put into holes with hot sulphur, which goes hard like cement, a common practice at the time. This accounts for the yellow around the rusting bolts that remain on Karekare Point now.

A few weeks after we arrived the light suddenly went out one night and

I went down with my father and Wally Farley to see what had happened. You will never guess what it was and this took place quite a bit in the years ahead. An eel had been swept along the flume into the tank and then down the jarrah pipe into the nozzle with a thud. The big pressure of water behind soon built up with no escape and this had to be stopped by going up to the top of the hill and lifting the flume out. With the water out the pipe took two hours to empty. This was given a speed up by turning on all the taps. As the pressure came away the nozzle could be made to unscrew and the remains of the eel fell into the water below.

At the back of the generator and under a lean-to, with a hole in the wall for the belt to go through, was the saw-bench and circular saw, also driven from the pelten wheel. As the days of the motorcar had not yet arrived, ti-tree, as it was cut, got put in the Konaki and taken over to the house and put into the woodbox. So you see it was the water that drove the saw that cut the wood that went in the box that heated the stove, heated the water for the baths and that cooked the meals not in the house that Jack built. Wally Farley would always say that no one could burn wood like his mother (my grandmother) and I can vouch for it in the hundreds of trees that I got down from the hills and cut up in the years to follow. That big stove would burn a ton a day going from 5 a.m. till 11 p.m. in the busy season and you got enough hot water for about 30 people to have a bath.

I had started at a new school at Karekare, not so far to go this time. Wally Farley's girl, Kathleen, was a year older than me and my brother Dudley just five years three months. Kathleen's brother, Wallace, who she called Woee, would be six in October, so us four were of school age, with the others all younger. Kathleen's mother, my Aunt Florrie, now arranged for

RIGHT The waterfall in flood, 1904.

MIDDLE Looking down the pipeline, 1937. This photo was taken from the tank looking down the 180 foot drop to the power-house below. The roof can be seen at the base of the pohutukawa tree.

TOP LEFT The waterfall and flume at the top, 1907.

BELOW Me at the sawbench cutting ti-tree, 1947.

I hold the head of Jewel Crest, given to me by my mother. This image was taken in the paddock in front of my cottage.

her sister Mona to come and teach us and things got going to a thunderous start. My father was driving the coach the day Mona arrived and on the way down the Karekare cutting the right front wheel collapsed and the coach slipped into the bank. As he struggled to quieten the horses Mona said, 'What are we going to do now?' his reply 'Get out quick.' With her out on the road he told her to hold the horses' heads while he got the traces undone and they both arrived home leading the horses.

As 1922 went by the others were getting older. John still had three years to go but Kathleen's sister, June, was five in May of that year, then came Neil and Douglas behind her.

Before the year was out it was decided to get two new coach horses and they were both black beauties we bought from Mr Sandel, a horse dealer in Mt Albert. They were called Darkey and Maud and both stood 16 hands. Darkey proved to be a wonder horse. Maud turned out to be good at bucking but no good for the coach so she was replaced in 1923 with another horse called Molly, also from Mr Sandel. Maud was sold to Harry Gibbons at Whatipu, a good horseman who said he would break her in for stock work.

The day after Darkey and Maud arrived, my father and Wally Farley put the saddles on them and went for a ride to try them out. Wally had Darkey and my father took Maud, but they did not go far for my father was no sooner in the saddle than she started to buck and he was thrown off with his foot caught in the stirrup, and dragged a bit before someone got hold of the bridle. I can't remember how they freed him but think with the bridle held probably by my grandfather, that Wally got down and undid the girth in the saddle. I know it gave my mother a fright as well as me and I kept wondering why he had hobnailed boots on. It was a lesson I never forgot and in later years when cattle mustering I always used my Texas saddle with Mexican bentwood stirrups that gave more room for your feet.

Soon the day arrived to put them in the coach, although Maud was not ridden again, she was now harnessed up beside Darkey with more fun and games. This time it was Darkey's turn and it was soon found that he would not stand still a second and was revving to go. As I watched I wondered how on earth the passengers were going to get into the coach. With Wally Farley at the reins and my father holding his head it took five or six minutes to get him still for a second while a passenger made a flying leap into the coach. It was just like a scene from the Warner Brothers great picture *Dodge City*, with the stagecoach about to leave except in this case up the Karekare Valley. Each time a passenger landed with a thud the whole performance had to be repeated while the next one got ready, even taking out their false teeth while preparing for a shove from behind. By the time the last one was on they were nearly down at the bridge and 20 to 25 minutes late getting away. Fortunately Maud did not try to buck but was pretty skittish and not letting Darkey have it all his own way.

Time was often made up as Darkey was just as keen to leave as he was to get home and being a fast walker he would pull the other horses as well as the coach if it did not keep up with him. His only fault was that he was hard to catch and it took three or four to corner him in a paddock. You had to gradually work up to his head, talking to him all the time and when he was ready he would turn his head to you and allow the bridle to be put on, but you had to be quick and not fumble with it. In a tribute to him he was the greatest coach horse we ever had and in earlier years I used him for stock work and could swing my seven foot stock whip over his head at full gallop, which made a bang like a .303 rifle, and his faith in me was such that he never even flicked an ear. To give you an idea of the position he was in, just before the bang came the lash was only six or eight inches above his head. I found him dead in the paddock one morning early in 1938 and buried him there. I am the only one who knows the position of his grave.

After Maud was sold to Harry Gibbons of Whatipu, Darkey's new mate was a big chestnut, 17 hands high, who we called Jimmy. I have only just remembered as I was going to bed last night and for the life of me cannot remember why he was not suitable in the coach. All I know is that my mother bought him and used to ride him so this meant that the horse dealer, Mr Sandel, had to find another one. He did, a bay mare who was called Molly, and she was the complete opposite to Darkey and did not suit him, but got pulled along by him till the end of the coaching days. She was

I hold my .303 rifle over Jewel Crest's head while my stockhorse, Peter, keeps his eyes on the camera. The building at the back is my mother and father's room. We stand in the spot where father was thrown off Maud.

Nervey the dog. Paratahi Island in the distance.

Taken at the end of Sandringham Valley, this image shows my mother holding my .303 rifle while her dog Codger, who looked just like Nervey, is resting beside her, 1937.

very quiet, easy to catch and came in handy for work with the sled. She was also used after we got our first car, a Model T Ford, to give it a pull up the Slippery Rock, the steepest part of the Karekare Cutting with a grade of one in four.

Like Darkey, I found her dead in the paddock one morning in 1940 and buried her where she lay, not far from the Norfolk pine that was planted by the grave of the girl belonging to Charles Murdoch who was drowned in the creek.

As I write this the light goes out and my first thought is an eel has gone down the pipe — no, the years have gone by and there is no more pipe for the eels to come down. Could it be that one of our modern drivers has had a power pole jump out at him? The poles never bothered us so could it be that beer and the winding West Coast Road that has plunged us into darkness?

Just across the creek to the left on the flat was a cottage called the Dunholm Cottage; the gully at the back going up to Mercers Bay was known as Dunholm Gully. Living in the cottage in 1927, when we arrived, were Mick Druble and his wife, and with them was a great pig dog that Mick called Nervey.

This dog took a great fancy to Wally Farley and would follow him all over the place. When they left and went to live in Takanini they took him with them and then kept him on a chain for a few days thinking he would settle down in his new home. As soon as he was let go he must have made straight for Karekare and the next morning when Wally got up here was Nervey at the door of his cottage. Mick came and got him and took him, again keeping him longer on the chain this time, but it was no good; as soon as he was let go he was back at Karekare the next day. So Mick told Wally he had better keep him. From now on Nervey took pride of place in all the pig hunting trips that were to follow over the years until his sad end in 1935.

On one occasion we had a boy of 17 called Erick working for us. As it was a Sunday morning he asked Wally Farley if he could have a loan of his .303 rifle, which he foolishly did. His girl, Kathleen, went with him and Nervey bailed a boar among the flax bushes on the top of Mt Zion. Kathleen got up into a flax bush out of the way and as soon as Erick saw it he got excited and fired without looking to see where Nervey was. Poor Nervey was on the other side of it and the big dumdum bullet tore through then came out and got Nervey in the front leg about three inches above his paw. Eric carried him home and had to tell Wally what he had done. The only thing to do was to put him out of his misery and Wally said he could not do it, so my father had to get his .22 rifle and take him round behind a sandhill. His grave is now buried under tons of sand and I alone know the spot. So from me a last tribute to Nervey, a great dog who loved the coast and the bush and twice found his way back to it all the way from Takanini.

Before closing the chapter on Nervey, I have one more story about him. I remember my father, with Wally Farley, was working on the Cutting and Nervey bailed a boar in the creek below. It was just before 5 a.m. and he kept it bailed by the little waterfall until after 5 p.m., when they went home for the gun.

This view from the top of Cave Rock shows Sandringham Valley. Dunholm Gully is in the top right-hand corner.

The Watchman and Karekare Point. In the distance is the top of Mt Zion, where Nervey was shot.

1920

Miss Bate and Herbert Perman

As we come to December 1922 it is my 8th birthday on the 11th and a girl from Tasmania called Miss Bate had come to work as a waitress for the summer. She had travelled round a lot and had a very pretty shell called a deep sea abalone, obtained only every seven years from the coast of California. She gave it to me saying, 'Happy birthday Wally, and I am sure you will look after it better than I can travelling round as I do.' That I have done and still have it, just as she gave it to me all those years ago.

Before she left us she met Herbert Perman, who had come out to cut ti-tree firewood for the next summer, and later married him, so her travels for a while did not get beyond the Waitakere Ranges. He lived in a white and green cottage just below Garlicks Bend, which was the sharp bend just where the West Coast Road joins Forest Hill Road. There was a store here, about 40 yards down Forest Hill Road, called Harnetts Store, which after the war became known as the Dutch Kiwi. They lived in this white and green cottage for a number of years and I cannot remember what happened to them. I have a faint recollection of waving to them when I started driving the West Coast Road.

The one thing I can remember about Herbert Perman is the hot tea he could drink. It never ceased to amuse me after I had boiled a billy for him when he was chopping on the 40-acre block above the Cutting gate, how quickly he could drink it down. So Miss Bate and Herbert Perman, like other early settlers, have passed on and I am probably the only one who remembers them now. I have the shell by the TV and with the reading light shining down on it, it looks quite pretty in the evening. What looks to be white is a silver colour with pale blue running through it.

1923

The Outlaw and *Te Toa*

In the winter of 1923 the road was so bad, with mud up to the hubs of the coach wheels, it was decided to leave the coach at home and ride one of the horses for the mail. My father and Wally Farley took turn-about each Thursday as it was always mail day. The horse they used was good old Darkey because he was such a fast walker.

I remember on several occasions riding my horse to meet my father on his way home. I usually met him between the Lone Kauri and Byles Flat. There was often a great deal of mail, postcards and forward bookings, there was also a lot of packages for the staff and mail order goods. Mother ordered a huge amount from catalogues, which all came out by mail. It was a case of walking home and leading Darkey, all smothered in mailbags. The first time I met him was just beyond Lone Kauri and all I could see of Darkey was his head and legs, the rest was a great heap of mailbags on the 15-mile walk home. A sample of the contents that got into these bags includes gramophone records, hobnail boots, baby's underwear, mother's and father's underwear and to top it off, the Farmers Trading Company had just started their 'free pair of hobnail boots with every half dozen blankets' offer. The Karekare Pony Express always came through.

Don't for one minute think that all this stuff came to just Karekare; bags and mail sacks needed to be dropped off all the way along the road at the different camps from Waiatarua onwards at The Nihotupu Dam, McElwains Flat, the Anawhata turn-off, Carters Hill, Darkey's Hill, Moff Byle's place, Lone Kauri and the Piha turn-off. All the other heavy goods such as sacks of flour, sugar, wheat, oats and chaff for the horses, had to come down from Onehunga to Whatipu on the launch, once a month. It then had to come along the beach on the Konaki, the sled being worked against the tide so as to get round the Karekare Point on the hard sand.

Waiting along the bank above the road for the mail, 1904. Second from left: Wally Farley, Helen Sugget, Marjorie Farley, Mrs Farley, Zoe Farley, unidentified, Laurie Farley's straw hat and Mrs Johnson.

The building of the Waitakere dams provided much employment for the area. Here the Lower Nihotupu Dam is officially opened.

The newly completed Upper Nihotupu Reservoir which flooded the Nihotupu Gorge all the way back to the much-visited Nihotupu Falls.

In later years the South Point got real bad and even at low tide the surf broke round it due to the shifting of the Manukau Bar. Often when this happened the four-wheel wagon had to be manhandled over Karekare Point rocks with one on each wheel and one holding the pole up. This was hard work, pulling over big stones and 9x9 sleepers where the engine used to run, and then turning it round with everyone holding on to the pole, lowering it down on to the beach on that side.

It was then a left turn at the point of Mt Zion. Everything had been unloaded and carried over the rocks. I remember all the trips just as if it was only yesterday. Leading the horses over the rocks with the traces hitched up round the collar, sometimes at 11 o'clock at night or later. Even now I can see the sparks flying from their shoes as they stepped over the greasy sleepers and struck the rocks on the other side. All this with the big rollers suddenly appearing out of the darkness and dashing on to the rocks in front and behind you.

Quite often Mr Laurie Farley came down with a benzene lantern, but this made things worse as the bright light shining on the pools of water lying in the rocks tended to dazzle you and the horses. I was 8½ years old. It was an all day job and the launch was quite often late and sometimes broke down, so we fished from the wharf to pass the time away. On the south side of Paratutui Island at Whatipu were a lot of loose stones and boulders and we used to sit there while boiling the billy for lunch. In those days the wharf on Paratutui was cut off at high tide and you could only get off at half or low tide.

The owner of the launch was Mr Wright, a big chap, over 6 feet tall. His first boat was called *The Outlaw*. She had no winch so all the loading and unloading had to be done by hand. I have seen him pick up a sack of maize, put it on his shoulder and step from the launch to the greasy wharf steps and then run up and dump it on top. One of his sons, 'Curly' as he was known, used to dive under the wharf for crayfish while the unloading was going on. He would go over the side and disappear in the green water and I would be thinking he was never going to come up, then suddenly he would appear with a crayfish in each hand and a knife in his teeth. He would fill several benzene boxes before they left on the return trip.

Wright Snr later got a larger launch called the *Te Toa*. She was a twin screw and had a winch, which was greatly appreciated by all who sailed on her or stood on the wharf while the heavy gear was lifted from the hold and swung over. As a little chap it fascinated me to hear the bell ring in the wheelhouse when all the passengers were safely on, with the ropes cast over as she would back away from the wharf.

The rip through the Manukau Heads on the outgoing tide is about 20 miles per hour; I used to watch *Te Toa* as she turned in to the channel and headed straight across to the harbour at Awhitu. It took her all her time to hold her own against the current, with the two engines going flat out. When she was just a speck in the distance it was time to put all the goods on a cart that ran on rails the length of the wharf. With this done it was about half-a-mile walk over the soft sand up to Gibbons' paddocks to get the horses harnessed and start the six-mile drive home along the beach.

The view from the South Point, looking back towards The Watchman. Just in front of the small stone surrounded by water is the spot that we used to haul the wagon up on to the rocks.

Quite often trips were made under less than ideal conditions. I have ridden the beach after a westerly gale and the foam would be right up to the girth of my horse.

One thing has always been a mystery to me and no early settler was ever able to give me a satisfactory reason for it. We were often driving along the beach in the dark and you could see the white waves out in the distance. It would be like this for quite a while and then suddenly, without any warning, the water would be halfway up the wheels, not just a wave or two, but the whole tide had come suddenly in on us. We were forced to turn up the beach on to the soft sand. After quarter of an hour or so it would all move out again into the dark distance, where it would remain for half an hour at least before having another go at us. I have thought a lot about it over the years as all those who experienced it with me are now gone, and believe me it was damned uncanny, so here I am left to supply the answer of answers for all you readers. It would only happen at night and I have never seen it in daylight.

Well all I can come up with is it must have something to do with the ancient past and the early Maoris had an answer for these things. So perhaps Kupe, who set out from his home near Tahiti about 925AD on a voyage that eventually brought him to New Zealand where he explored both islands. It is said he stopped on his way up the West Coast of the North Island at Manukau Heads where, at a certain rock now known as The Nine Pin, he performed the ritual necessary for a successful passage on Whare Hukahuka o Tangaroa, 'The Sea God's Foamy Dwelling'. This rock is today battered by the surf that rolls in from the Tasman Sea, but in Kupe's time, the saying is that it rose up from a low sandy plane that extended seawards and was covered in clumps of manuka and flax. Could it then be that the Sea God in his foamy dwelling was causing big surges from this vanished land?

Curly Wright later became skipper of the *Te Toa* so he certainly didn't have much time to dive for crayfish. Some opposition arrived in the name of a Mr White and his new launch, the *Awhitu*.

I remember one afternoon at Whatipu with big surf on the bar and the high tide running out. *The Outlaw* broke down mid-channel. It was touch and go for sure as she was drifting out towards the bar, so the *Awhitu* had to come to her rescue and tow her all the way back to Onehunga.

92   The Iron-Bound Coast

By 1930 trade in the Manukau had fallen away to such an extent that they decided to take the *Te Toa* out over the bar and round the North Cape, then down the east coast to the Bay of Plenty. Curly skippered her until she neared Tauranga but while sheltering from a storm she dragged the anchor and went on to the rocks before Curly could get the engines going. That was the end of the *Te Toa* and poor Curley Wright, who was drowned in the wreck. *The Outlaw*, saved from the foamy dwelling of Whare Hukahuka o Tangaroa, continued to ply the Manukau for several years after *Te Toa* had gone. Both boats served well in these pioneering years of the twenties and thirties.

As the summer of 1923 continued, the road dried out and the coach went back on the run to Waikumete. The heavy goods still came down to Whatipu so the beach trips continued. The other children used to go for a swim in the lagoon after school, but I had to go up on Karekare Point for the cows each day, so only got an occasional dip. I did find a few skulls at the base of The Watchman when I went down on my own to cool down after getting back to the stockyard. These had been uncovered by 'hauaauru', the west wind.

My grandparents and others had told me that it was Hone Heke who came down the coast in his war canoes and attacked the pa at Karekare, killing all but one. This young warrior survived the massacre by climbing down the seaward face of The Watchman and hiding in clumps of pohutukawa till after dark. He then made his way along the beach to Whatipu and later crossed over to Awhitu.

This daytime photo gives some idea of what it would be like in the dark when Whare Hukahuka o Tangoroa seemed to object to us being on his beach.

The latter part was correct but it was not Hone Heke but another Ngapuhi chief called Tareha, who wiped out the pa. In later years I had talked with Pa Bethell, William Foote (who had the mill at Pararaha in the 1870s), Abel Lovett and others, who all said it was Tareha. The story, as was told to me, goes as follows.

After the musket-armed Ngapuhi had defeated Ngati Whatua in the big battle near Kaiwaka, Tareha led a war party to the Kaipara and then down the west coast. The largest pa were Hihurongi [sic] and Karekare, both situated on high land. When the tribe at Karekare heard that he was on his way down the coast and war canoes were sighted in the distance by lookouts, they hid their tribal and ceremonial treasures in the bush. They then retreated inside their pa on top of The Watchman. The war canoes came through the surf and landed on the beach at the foot of The Watchman.

The battle was on, but the local tribe had no chance against the heavily armed attackers. Tareha was said to be a huge man weighing about 30 stone. His partiality to human flesh was well known and no doubt at Karekare his appetite was satisfied for a while. His plan was to starve them out and this he did as they had left themselves with no way of getting more food or water. As they became weaker he took some of his warriors and forced his way up on top, where he threw them all over to the warriors waiting on the beach below. So the skulls I found were from those that he had thrown from the top.

I have often thought of all The Watchman has witnessed while standing there; and I could hear hauaauru, the west wind, who takes a delight in whisking the sparkling foam from the tops of the breakers, bending and twisting the trees to fantastic shapes, or flattening the manuka scrub on the seaward slopes as it dashes past.

My mother told me that in 1900, when my grandfather bought the place from Charles Murdoch, that Mr Murdoch told them that the young warrior who managed to climb down the face of The Watchman returned one day as an old man and said that he had come back to die. This was in 1889, three years after Murdoch had bought the place from John and Silas Shaw. Murdoch said the old chap was around for a while and then one morning they found he was missing and never saw him again. Being the sole survivor of the massacre he would feel that he must come back to the place where they all died. They thought that he had gone to the place where the treasure was buried, but I have other ideas and never got the chance to follow them up. I am getting old myself, but still think I know the answer and will let him rest in peace.

Karekare Creek and The Watchman, 1896.

1924

At the start of 1924 I had just turned nine and apart from going up to Karekare Point each day after school in the hot sun for the cows, I also had to go up the flax gully and all round the top of Mercer's Bay before breakfast. The cows were let go all the time then I would walk miles before and after school tracking them through the bush. Those that wandered the most had a bell round their neck but they got so canny that if they heard me or the dog they would stand still so it would not ring. I had the help of my father's first dog, a black one called Spark, and had just been given my first stock whip, which I soon learned to crack with perfection.

With winter coming on it meant the road getting bad again and having to ride for the mail, so the coach got a spell. When it was my father's turn to go and if the cows did not give me a lot of trouble after school, I would saddle up and go to meet him, taking some of the load from Darkey.

One day a week was usually kept for pig hunting and we used to mainly go up the Taraire Gully as far as The Company (named from the timber mill days) to just below what is now Lone Kauri Farm stream. The Taraire Gully was then just a rough track; during the thirties it was widened and known as Six Foot Track, now it is the new road. If we had not had any luck we would work over to the head of the Pararaha, then back into the Taraire Gully or out on to the top of Mt Zion.

My mother and Aunt Florence would have an afternoon a week to go fishing as we usually had plenty of wild pork and fish through the winter months. Some of the visitors would say, 'Whatever do you people do with yourselves in winter?' I'd tell them, 'Oh, we just laugh and talk about the funny people we see in the summer.'

There was now talk of a motorcar to come before Christmas and in all the excitement I noticed that even the horses had pricked up their ears. November came at last and the big day was upon us, rushing in with the dawn like a spring tide. Everyone was up with the birds, not the crack of dawn as it was a beautiful day and the birds all had feathers and were chirping away, making the most of it while the kids' mouths were coping with breakfast.

The part I remember well was having boiled custard with the sweets for the midday dinner. This must have been a reward for doing so much, for so long, for so many. Even now after all these years I can still see my Aunt Florrie pouring it on before she handed it to me.

There was a continual procession backwards and forwards to the veranda for a look up the valley while others were climbing up on the lawn gate for a better view. At last it was spotted on top of the hill before the Cutting gate. Then with several toots on the horn it came along the flat over the bridge and stopped in front of the house. Here it was, a shiny new 1924 Model T Ford with a busybody at the back where eight people sat, four each side facing one another and one beside the driver.

In the car, which now makes history as our first motorcar, was a man from the Ford Company who drove it out, and my grandfather, Wally Farley, and my father. The man stayed a few days while Wally Farley mastered the art of handling the car. You could no longer say 'whoa', or 'get up there', as had been done for countless ages.

The Model T

For all those who know nothing about driving a Model T Ford, perhaps I should explain the art of this bygone era. On the floor in front of you were three pedals. On the left was the low gear, one which worked in conjunction with the handbrake and you only had a hand throttle. In the middle was the reverse one and on the right the footbrake. These pedals all had to be held down to keep in gear. You can imagine what it was like on your foot holding the low gear down for two miles while climbing the Karekare Cutting. When you could get out of low gear you just sped up with the hand throttle, took your foot off the pedal and shifted the handbrake at the same time from the neutral position to the right-hand one. With the long climb out of the valley, the worst feature was not only holding down the pedal but the fact that on the steep part-slippery rock (with no vacuum tank) she could not suck the petrol up from the tank at the back. It was evident after that first trip one of the horses would have to be taken ahead to wait at the bottom of the Slippery Rock and then be hitched on to give it a pull up that part. This job fell to my father and Molly.

My father on Molly just after hitching on at the bottom of Slippery Rock. In front of the Model T, Wally Farley and a lady passenger (1925).

This job had to be done every Thursday and the passengers had to get out and push as well. When the group got to the top, all out of breath and gasping for air, Wally would put his head outside and say, 'My word we did well to get up there'.

I remember on several occasions when they got to Waikumete my father would have to get on the train and go into town and get two new tyres, then get the train back again. He and Wally Farley would then have to fit them before returning home. Just think of it, the tread all gone from the back tires in one trip.

Apart from no vacuum tank, the Ford had a steering that was simply out of this world, or just on the edge of it since the dawn of time. This was caused by a single spring mounted crosswise above the axle and known as transverse springing. This was the cause of the steering being so tricky and it took only a stone the size of an egg to whip the wheel right out of your hand. Another peculiarity related to their being no vacuum tank was to turn round at the foot of a hill and back up so the petrol would run down to the carburettor. Many a motorist who did not have a Model T was on the verge of having his eyesight tested after seeing one going up a hill while facing him and getting farther away all the time.

It was during all these trials and tribulations that Wally came up with the Twenty Ford Psalm while endeavouring to get up the Cutting. 'The Ford is my car, I shall not want another. It maketh me to lie down in wet places, it leadeth me beside the still water table. It sourest my soul, it leadeth me in the path of trouble. For its name sake, yea thou it run down the valleys it is towed up the hills. It angers me in the presence of mine enemies, it anointed my head with oil, its tank runneth over. Surely the darn thing shall not follow me all the days of my life, or I dwell in the house of the insane forever.' We all had several trips to town when the Christmas rush was over, but the enthusiasm soon wore away when everyone had to get out at the bottom of Slippery Rock and push.

My brother John, 1921.

Wild surf around Paratahi Island.

1925

Before Easter and winter could rush at us again, it was thought surely there must be something better than a Model T Ford, and there was. A chance remark sent my father and Wally Farley to Dominion Motors in Albert Street, Auckland City, and here was the answer: a wonderful car, a 1925 6-cylinder Essex. It looked quite capable of doing what they said it could.

I can't remember if the Model T went back or if it was traded in on the Essex. Anyway, a few days after the visit to Dominion Motors the Essex arrived and here was a car indeed. No more pedals to hold down; it had the luxury of a gear lever and it stayed where it was put.

My father kept his riding boots but gave up his saddle and Molly was keen to have a look at the new motorcar that could climb hills on its own. Father's boots were now required for a new technique; going up into the bush and cutting pongas and ti-tree for 'foreseens' to be laid across the big holes, so the wheels would not sink out of sight. My father and Wally now made clear that an attempt was going to be made to get through all the winters.

So, every Thursday, which just happened to be mail day, and with chains on the back wheels and an axe, slash hook and spade inside plus gumboots for good measure, they were ready to leave at 9 a.m. My father found the front seat a better saddle. If you look at the photo carefully you can just see the chains on the back wheels.

We all watched them go and wondered how they would get on but knew it would be hours before we got any news and that was only if they gave a ring from Harnetts Store on the corner of West Coast Road and Forest Hill Road. If they got that far they would be on the metal road and a downhill run to Glen Eden and the station.

They did not call but we got a call Mr Neville Ussher's place at the top of the Piha Hill when a horseman going to Piha asked them to ring and say that they had only got as far as Lone Kauri by 2 o'clock and were going to

The 1925 Essex up to the axle in mud on McElwain's Flat, 1925. I later drove this car, in the same conditions, from 1930–32.

From left: Mr Ted Browne, who had just come to Karekare to live, my father, and Mr Jim Lockett from Piha. They are clearing a tree that fell across the road, 1925.

Pat Cole

Pat Cole was an Irishman who had come to work for us at Easter and liked the place so much that he wanted to stay on through the winter.

In the spring I remember going down to look at the state of Karekare Point with my mother, brother Dudley and Pat Cole. After we had been there a while the tide looked as if it was going to be extra low and was still falling. I said to my mother as we walked out towards Paratahi, 'It looks as if we might be able to get on to it soon.' As we got to it and were only about 30 yards away, I started to walk out and called out to the others, 'Come on, it's only ankle deep.' We got on and Pat and I went round on to the seaward side for a quick look. I noted that the tide had turned, so called to him come on back. It was unique, for in the 29 years I lived at Karekare we were never able to reaccomplish it again. Must have been one of those rare tides that occur every 18 years. It's now an almost yearly occasion and the massive build-up of sand makes it possible to walk out on a strip of sand most winter low tides.

try to turn round and come back. The road was a sea of mud; if by chance you accidentally hit yourself on the head with one of the big pongas while putting it under the wheels you would drown in the sea of mud and slush. Such was motoring in 1925. They arrived home in time to do the milking and call it a day.

The next week it was back to boots and saddle again and Wally Farley left with Darkey at 5 a.m. It was decided to take the Essex only if the road had a chance to dry out for a few days, but as winter was now closing in on the valley and shaking his wet coat all over New Zealand, there was not much chance of this. A few times that winter they managed to get as far as McElwains Flat and a truck from Glen Eden brought the mail and goods that far. Then it would be back to Darkey again.

About July the cows were starting to calve. We had a Jersey-cross with long sharp horns called Brindle, and she had been put in the calf paddock that led into the stockyard a few days before she had her calf. After the calf was born she became much wilder than the previous year, so much so that she would even charge a bird if it settled in the paddock near her.

The idea was to get her into the stockyard; looking the situation over it was decided that Wally Farley would have to go up one side of the fence and my father with Pat the Irishman would take the other side. On my father's side and inside the fence was a drain about three feet deep and four feet wide. They had all gone about 20 yards when Brindle, who had been watching closely from the top of the paddock, decided that was close enough and dropped her head and charged. They all tried to get through the fence, but my father and Pat Cole had to jump the drain first and Pat slipped and fell in, breaking his leg close to the knee. As my father and Wally had both got through the fence and Pat had disappeared from sight, Brindle stopped and went back to her calf.

Now what to do. It was decided my grandfather would go up towards her on the outside of the fence to attract her attention but not get too close. My father and Wally would then go into the paddock and try to get Pat out. When my grandfather was in position and had her closely watching him, the other two went into the paddock and worked forwards cautiously. Brindle turned to face the new threat and watched both parties at the same time, so Wally called out, 'Hang your coat on the fence and move back.' The cow kept her eyes on the coat for a while and then decided it could not do much harm so turned to see if Pat was still in the drain or what the other two might come up with. In the meantime the calf was asleep behind a small bush.

After one more attempt my father said to Wally, 'I think you had better go and get the gun,' so he went to his cottage and came back with his 12-bore shotgun. They started to go again, with Wally carrying the gun, but they had not gone far before Brindle decided the coat was no problem, my grandfather was too far way to be a problem; so she decided to fix the two closest to her. She dropped her head and charged. They both got through the fence and Wally turned and fired at her, breaking one front leg. Back she went to the calf and they soon found she could come down the paddock on three legs nearly as fast as four. Finally it was decided someone would go up the opposite side to my grandfather and hammer some sticks into the ground.

In the meantime Pat, lying in the drain, wondered what was going on. The next thing on the programme was, while the sticks were being hammered in, for my grandfather and the other person to keep calling out and talking about anything. Quite some time had passed since Pat fell into the drain and it began to look as if they were preparing a cricket patch to distract the ever increasingly angry cow. A discussion took place, with much shouting from both sides of the paddock, and my father kept shouting to me to keep back; I had already picked a strong tree to sit in.

Brindle still defied all attempts to get to Pat and kept a sharp watch on everything, including birds.

My father, thinking this over, said to Wally, 'She will have to be shot.' But Wally didn't have any more cartridges and said my father would, 'have to try and drop her with your .22 rifle.' My father crept his way up through

This photo shows me with a bull-calf and my cattle dog, Wolf. This is the spot where Brindle had her calf.

the pohutukawa trees on the right-hand side to get as close as possible for a shot between the eyes or behind the ear. After about a quarter of an hour he got his chance and dropped her.

All the men carried Pat out on a camp stretcher and he had to be put on the backseat of the Essex and taken to the hospital. Remember the state of the roads and the task that lay ahead to get him to the metal which was beyond McElwains Flat? Just think of the car swinging violently from side to side in the deep ruts as Wally tried to get the Essex up The Cutting around the Slippery Rock, the Lone Kauri ruts, up Darkey's Hill, Devils Elbow, City Council Notice Flat, bouncing into Hen Coup Bend, Carters Hill and then McElwains Flat. What would any one today say if they had to go through that?

After an awful struggle they got Pat to the hospital where he was for about eight weeks, I think. He had to have a silver plate put in his leg and the day before he was due to come back to Karekare, while getting round the ward on crutches, it gave way and he had to go through the whole performance again. He was pretty down in the dumps and they got a ring from the hospital to that effect, so my father, mother, Wally and Aunt Florrie thought they better try to get through to see him. To make a long story short they did, but the visiting hours were long past when they eventually got there and the hospital staff had all said their prayers and gone to bed. They saw one of the nurses and explained that they had been all day trying to get there from the West Coast. She was sympathetic but said the visiting hours were long past but would see a Charge Sister. They all felt they must impress her. The situation was serious as all four of them made it quite plain that they did not intend to go until they had seen Pat. Finally, it was agreed they could see him. The nurse went to his ward and asked, 'Are you awake Mr Cole? Your cousins are here from the coast.' There was great excitement in the ward, those who had gone to sleep woke up and couldn't believe their eyes, here was a chap who was nearly dead when they went to sleep, laughing his head off, surrounded by people covered in mud, hours after visiting time was over. Eventually Pat got back to Karekare and while he was recuperating was involved with another cattle round-up with a mob of bullocks thrown in for good measure.

This photo of me was taken outside the stockyard in 1937.

Sammy — a gift from Neptune

I have told of how the cattle from the wreck of the barque *Orwell* swum ashore from the Manukau Bar in March 1848. This remarkable swim was also made by a great dog in 1925, who was found on the beach exhausted, by my cousin Kathleen (hence the title, 'A gift from Neptune'). She went back and got her father, Wally Farley, to come back and help carry him back. She said she thought he had been washed off a scow that may have had cattle on board.

After a few days rest the dog was taken for the cows and soon demonstrated his capability in this respect. We gave him the name of Sammy, which he seemed to like. Although he was someone's great loss he knew he had found a good home after that long swim.

It was not long before I would go up on The Watchman at 3 o'clock, look over the bay to Karekare Point and say, 'Sammy, go and get the cows.' Off he would go across the sand, then through Sandringham Valley and right up into the saddle on Karekare Point. I used to watch him go into the top of the watercourse then come out the other side and work his way round the top of the saddle so as to get behind the cows. He knew how many there were and just before getting down into the Sandringham Valley they would use two different tracks, so he would check both to see that they had gone right through and not dodged him. Some of them were very cunning and would take the bottom track and stop halfway through, while the others went by on the top track. I pointed this out to him on the first trip when I was with him and he then knew what to do.

Unfortunately he only had a few years of working life left as he was not a young dog and he began to lose his teeth and his eyesight failed him. He would put his nose to the ground to find them that way. At that time we used to kill our own mutton and he would round up the sheep using his nose. When the time came for him to retire I had to take over again and cover ground each day with another younger dog not as capable.

The place on the beach where Sammy swam ashore from the Manukau Bar

Part of Sandringham Valley, 1896.

Mr Bob Gordon

Bob Gordon had come from England, but while working in South Africa lost his right arm in a mining accident. He then came to New Zealand but returned to England to marry a girl he knew there, bringing her back to New Zealand, and settled on a farm at the Huia. While farming he was also working the bush and getting the kauri out that had been left in more awkward spots from the earlier mill days, with bullocks.

Arthur Baker

Arthur Baker was also a great horseman and all-round bushman. Anything to do with horses, cattle, bush work or pig hunting, you would find him in the thick of it. He always rode a flighty horse about 17 hands and was as hard as nails.

About six months after I knew him, while working in the bush with the bullocks one day, a log rolled and crushed the bone in his hip to a pulp. It was a hard job to get him to hospital where he stayed for 22 weeks. The doctors were told that he was a great horseman, but told him that he would never be able to ride a horse again and that one leg would be shorter than the other.

After a week back at Huia he was to report to the doctor's again, so got Mrs Gordon to help him catch his horse and put the saddle on. He then got his big chestnut up against a bank while he got on and Mrs Gordon handed him one of his crutches, which he took with him, and headed off to hospital. He rode as far as New Lynn, left his horse there and got the train into town. The doctor was very pleased with the progress he had made and went on to remind him of what he had said, that he would never be able to ride again. With that Arthur casually remarked, 'Oh, I have just ridden in from Huia this morning.' The doctor just about collapsed and would have taken a hell of a lot of reviving if he had seen the horse that was waiting at New Lynn for the return journey to the Huia.

After getting clearance from his doctor, Arthur was back in action again at Huia. He overcame the shorter leg by riding his horse alongside the bullocks and directing them through the bush. He would call out, 'Come on Mousey, get into it Tiger,' and so on. As each bullock knew his name it would respond to the call even though Arthur was mounted on a horse. He still had his long whip, which he would crack over the bullock's back as he called its name to induce more effort into the pull.

To see a team in action was an interesting sight and the individual bullocks had a useful life of about four years, after which they were fattened for market. For training a fresh bullock, it was yoked alongside a trained one and after it had tried to escape from the wooden yoke that connected it to its mate, it would settle down and become a member of the team. In some cases only a day was needed to tame them.

One day while mastering cattle, the dogs bailed a wild pig in the creek below the road. Arthur got off his horse, tied it up and on hands and knees went down the bank. He then managed to grab the hind legs of the pig and put his boot on its head to drown it, as he had lost his knife on the way down. To get back to the road and his horse he had to crawl up the bank, through the bush, dragging the pig after him. Up on the road he got back on his horse and went home for a sledge.

Twelve months after all this drama, he was skinning a sheep under a tree, the ground was wet as it had been raining, and he slipped and fell, putting out his hand to save himself. There must have been a box nailed to the tree at some time; the box had rotted away leaving the rusty nail, which went right into the palm of his hand. They had to pull him off and get him to hospital and I'm sorry to say that three days later he was dead with blood poisoning. So, I write it all now as a tribute to a great horseman, bushman and pioneer of more than half a century ago.

By the Kakamatua Stream or 'Cochamatoa' as it was called by the locals, a large sawmill operated in the 1860s and 1870s. In 1850 Mathew Roe was cutting the kauri and rafting the logs up to his mill at Onehunga.

Now it was the turn of Bob Gordon and Arthur Baker. In 1925 they began to work out what the others had left with bullocks. I remember the names of two of the bullocks, Mousey and Tiger. Bob had over 20 big strong bullocks. When they were not being worked he would bring them from Huia to Whatipu and along the beach to Karekare to go up on Karekare Point for grazing.

I had seen Mrs Kathleen Gordon bring them all round on her own with three dogs and timed it so as to arrive at The Karekare Point at low tide. You can imagine the noise as they all had bells on when not working so they could be found in the bush when wanted again. She often did this if the men were busy in the bush and thought no more of it than sitting down to the table for a meal. For an English girl she took to the life like a duck to water. This was no mean feat to bring over 20 bullocks along the 4 miles of rough clay road between Huia and Whatipu and then 6 miles along the beach with just the help of three dogs. She must have been a tremendous help to Bob as she could also kill and skin a sheep. Riding was also one of her great accomplishments and she could manage any horse, including Bob's big stock horse, Pewelka.

This horse used to give Bob a lot of trouble at times, with his one arm, and he was that sort of horse that couldn't stand to see another horse in front of him. So when he was rounding up cattle on his own, if another horseman appeared in the distance Pewelka took off like a rocket leaving Bob's cattle to scatter in all directions. It was also no mean feat to ride a horse with one arm. He would take the reins in his teeth while cracking the stock whip with his left hand, galloping over uneven ground at the same time.

One day my father was on Karekare Point looking out for some of our cattle and saw a wild cow and calf in among all the bullocks. He decided the only way to get her was to drive them all down to the stockyard. As I mentioned before, these bullocks

This photo, taken in 1896, shows The Point in the background, where the bullocks were put to graze in 1925.

A wild bull, a descendant from the *Orwell* accident, and the man who shot it, Arthur White.

had bells on, not ordinary cow bells but big bullock bells that could be heard for miles. So you can imagine the noise as they all came over the sand on to the flat behind the dance hall, this wild cow and calf in with them. I was at school then and had just come out for playtime as my father started shouting to open the stockyard gate. After they were all in the yard came the job of getting the calf away from the cow. They all kept milling round and round for quite a while and then the calf was grabbed as it came near the gate. A rope was then thrown over the horns of the cow, but the gate came open with the pressure against it and all the bullocks started to come out. The cow saw the opening and made a dash for it and with my father, grandfather and Wally Farley all hanging on to the rope; she dragged them down the drive in front of the house. Each time she tried to charge them they put the dogs on her and gradually got right along the road as far as the first paddock. It was then seen to be useless so Wally went for the gun and shot her. It is of interest to note that she was the last wild cow I saw that was a direct descendant of those cattle from the barque *Orwell*, wrecked on the Manukau Bar on 2 March 1848.

They decided to get the horse on the Konaki sled to take the dead cow down to the beach to be buried. As they left the house Pat Cole got in and was sitting at the back by the tailboard. When they got near, the sight of the dead cow on the road was too much for Molly, who quickly turned round in the traces and jumped right into the Konaki. A somewhat startled Pat did a roll over the tailboard on to the road. Molly was standing in the Konaki with her back to the dead cow, watching Pat favouring his leg while getting the hell out of it.

The next day Bob Gordon came along and I showed him the calf. He took a few steps towards it and said, 'Come on little sukie.' It dropped its head, opened its mouth and charged right at him, bowling him over. I decided to call this calf Wildfire, it was a heifer and I reared her on the bucket, but she always had a wild streak in her that got worse over the years. The first year after she had her calf we milked her with the others and she handled quite well. The second year she began to get a bit troublesome when she started to kick and send the bucket flying. We did not bail the cows, but milked them in the yard where they stood. I accidentally found the way to handle her. I pretended that I did not know the others were watching and wondering why I did not get kicked. In the third year I was milking her twice a day. One morning I was looking for two cows that were missing and one of the others tried to milk Wildfire, with destructive effect, getting kicked in the shin, and the bucket didn't fare any better. When I got back with the two culprits I was told what had happened and my father said, 'I think we will have to get rid of her. What are we going to do if you are away or sick?' I said, 'Yes, I suppose we will have to get Bob Gordon to put a price on her next time he is round.' She had one peculiar marking — something that I will always remember — it was a white patch that looked just like the map of Australia on her left front leg, high up on the shoulder, which was red.

A few days later Bob Gordon came round to see if we had any cattle for sale and said he had some to pick up at Whatipu on the way back. We had several and my father asked how much Wildfire was worth. I was sorry to see her go in a way as I had reared her on the bucket from the day her mother was shot. Precaution was now the order of the day as Bob decided to go and have a look at her from the outside fence. Several pohutukawa trees provided good cover for a closer look and he said to me, 'You come with me as she knows you.' We set off and the others followed at a distance. Wildfire looked up and saw me, no doubt wondering who Bob was, not remembering charging him when she was a calf. It was not necessary to go any closer and he said, '£7 10 shillings 8 pence,' which was a good price then. I went down to the Point with him when he left and the last I saw of Wildfire was heading along the beach to Whatipu with a bunch of cattle. At Pararaha she would be on the exact spot where those cattle she was descended from had swum ashore from the wreck of the *Orwell* in March 1848.

I had many droving trips with Bob Gordon in the following years and was with him at the Henderson stockyards on the Monday morning of 8 December 1941 when the news came through that the Japanese had attacked Pearl Harbour. I had the biggest bunch of steers I had ever reared at that sale and at a good price. People kept coming up to me and saying, 'A nice bunch of cattle, Wally,' and, 'You did well today.'

This photo of me shows how we used to milk cows where they stood in the yard.

Some of the cattle on the beach, with the Hereford bull on the right. They're all looking in the direction Wildfire had gone.

Boy lost in Mercers Bay

It was on one morning in the spring of 1925 that I got up early to get the cows and found a strange man outside in a distressed state. After a while I managed to get his story and found out what had happened. Apparently he and his 14-year-old son had set out to climb along the edge of the cliffs from Piha to Whatipu. While going round the edge of Mercers Bay the boy had put his hand on a rock that pulled out and he fell to his death. The father had managed to climb down and spent the night with the body and at daylight had left to try and get help.

Mercers Bay is a treacherous place for those who don't know it. Everything is loose and likely to pull out if you catch hold of it, and this is just what happened. In those days the only way down was at the northern end of the beach on Mr Neville Ussher's property and this was done by climbing down a slippery watercourse.

The first thing my father did when I called him was to ring the police station at Henderson. Constable Douglas came out and made arrangements for the hearse to come to Karekare.

It was decided that several men would go down the watercourse, get the body and bring it round the rocks to a place opposite our fishing rocks. There is quite a gap here, separated by very rough water at most times. The job was now to get the body across this gap and up on to our fishing rocks, which at this spot was called the 'balcony'. The only way was to get a rope across from the balcony to the men at Mercers Bay. But how? I was able to provide an answer with my bow and

In this photo you can see the treacherous gap that the boy's body had to get across to be on the balcony of the fishing rocks in the foreground. The arrow landed where the waves are breaking in the centre. In the background are Shag Rock, Mercers Bay and in the far distance, Whites Point, Piha.

arrows; the bow made from lancewood and the arrows were bamboo with turkey feathers at the base.

My father took them and, with my grandfather Wally and the driver of the hearse, went down to the fishing rocks. A hole was made in the arrow behind the turkey feathers and a light fishing line was tied to it. I am not sure if it was my father or Wally Farley who shot the arrow over, but they kept plenty of slack so that the end could be tied to the rope they had with them. The arrow landed in the cleft of the rock and was retrieved by those in Mercers Bay when the waves went back. They were Constable Douglas and the father of the boy, who was nearly frantic with what he would face with the boy's mother when he got back.

After they had retrieved the arrow those on the balcony of the fishing rocks tied the line to the rope, which was pulled over and the body tied to it. Then it was a matter of pulling it back. The hardest part was to come; lifting it from the water that was about 30 feet below them. Fortunately the sea was not that rough.

They carried the body, which was wrapped in sacks, from the beach and once again it was to be Molly and the Konaki to get it up to the hearse at the house.

Constable Douglas and the boy's father then had to climb back up the watercourse and out of the bay. What the man told his wife when he got home I do not know, but even at the age of 10 I could not understand how any man from the city could be so stupid as to take a boy into a place like that.

A photo taken from the northern end of Mercers Bay, looking south. The watercourse the rescuers went down is just out of sight, at the bottom. In the distance are the sheer cliffs with our property at the top, and Shag Rock, the Long Rocks and the Fishing Rocks with the waves dashing on to the balcony and Cave Rock. In the distance, Paratahi Island.

To have and to hold and then to be sold

It was with some regret that I have now come to the part where this is to be recorded along with all the other events, and the contributing factor was of course the state of the road. Ever since he bought the place in 1900, my grandfather had been striving to get the road metalled, which was an endless bog hole in the winter. Frequent trips to the Waitemata Council always brought the same answer. 'You are the only ratepayers out that far

---

The visit of the American battle fleet, 1925

In 1925 the Waitemata Harbour was full of American battleships and a great sight to see. I think it was August for it was school holidays and my father and Wally Farley spent days putting pongas across the bogs so we could all get in to see them.

The Californian was the flagship and she was alongside Princess Wharf. I went on her first with my father, mother, and brothers Dudley and John, but they would not remember anything of it. We stayed in a boarding house called The Chimes in Symonds Street and the next day went on the *Colorado* and *West Virginia*. What stunned us was the luxury on the warships: ice water fountains everywhere and huge steam presses so each man could have his uniform pressed twice a day.

I will never forget one episode as I stood on the deck of the *Colorado* and watched another boatload coming alongside. Just as it got near the ladder it suddenly sped up and rushed away. Round it came again, then back for another go, but the same thing happened again. By this time some of the passengers were getting very annoyed as they had come a long way and wanted to get on the *Colorado*, not play musical boats. One angry woman could be heard shouting at the launchman; 'What do you think you are doing, damn your blasted boat!'

The trouble was the clutch was slipping . The woman was shouting about the blasted boat and the launchman replied, 'I can't help it lady, my clutch is slipping.' 'I don't want to hear about your blooming clutch.' Of course they didn't get on the *Colorado* and I don't know if they had to keep going round till they ran out of petrol to get back to the wharf.

I can remember for certain the names of some of the others: *Maryland, Pennsylvania, Iowa, New Mexico, Arizona* (sunk at Pearl Harbour), *Nevada, Wisconsin* and *Mississippi*. I told this joke to some of the Americans I met in Guadalcanal during the war and they said I was damn clever. 'If Mississippi and Missouri gave Massachusetts a New Jersey, what would Delaware? Idaho but I'll Alaska.'

and we do not have the money.' His reply to this was that the road passed through a large area in the Nihotupu Valley known as The Watershed on which no rates were paid. The Nihotupu Dam, at the centre of The Watershed, has a surfaced area of 36 acres and was completed in 1923.

My father returned home from his last visit to the county office with what seemed to him the only answer: more ratepayers for the county. I overheard the plan, which was to sell sections all along the valley above the road and up on The Watchman, with dismay. Though only 10 years old, I voiced my concern for the factors and realised then as I have all my life that you cannot overcome one problem by creating another. Having been the first ones to own both sides of the valley and all the beach to the high water mark, the first step in the slide away had been when my father gave a road right through the property to the boundary at Mt Zion.

With the sections on The Watchman this meant another road would have to be given up the side of the calf paddock, round the top of it, then right through the middle of the property to come out by Mr Neville Ussher's place on the Piha Road. So you can now see the picture developing as I saw it, a good road, and baches galore. Piha had started to attract buyers for section and, before we knew it, the whole place was for sale. What the place would be worth today if it had all been kept private! Just think of it, 500 acres of prime coastal land and a mile of ocean beach with riparian rights, the second oldest electrical plant in this country operating before Auckland, plus the hidden treasure of the ancient Kawerau tribe.

The sections were to be sold by auction and I think it was about October 1925. The first two on The Watchman were bought by a lawyer, Mr Jack Mansell, for £75; these are the only ones that I can remember the price paid.

The Watchman, 1925. The sections that were to be sold ran from just behind the pohutukawa tree to the foot of the steep part of the hill.

The last one on The Watchman, at the foot of the steep part, was bought by a Mr Gamlin, but I can't remember the price paid. The third one along the road from the house was bought by a builder called Lyons, whose home was built by one of his men, a Mr Bullford, with help from Lyons at times. He then got into financial trouble and it came back on Mrs Farley's hands about six months later, who later left it to me in her will. The one next to it, the fourth, was bought by a school teacher from Te Kuiti.

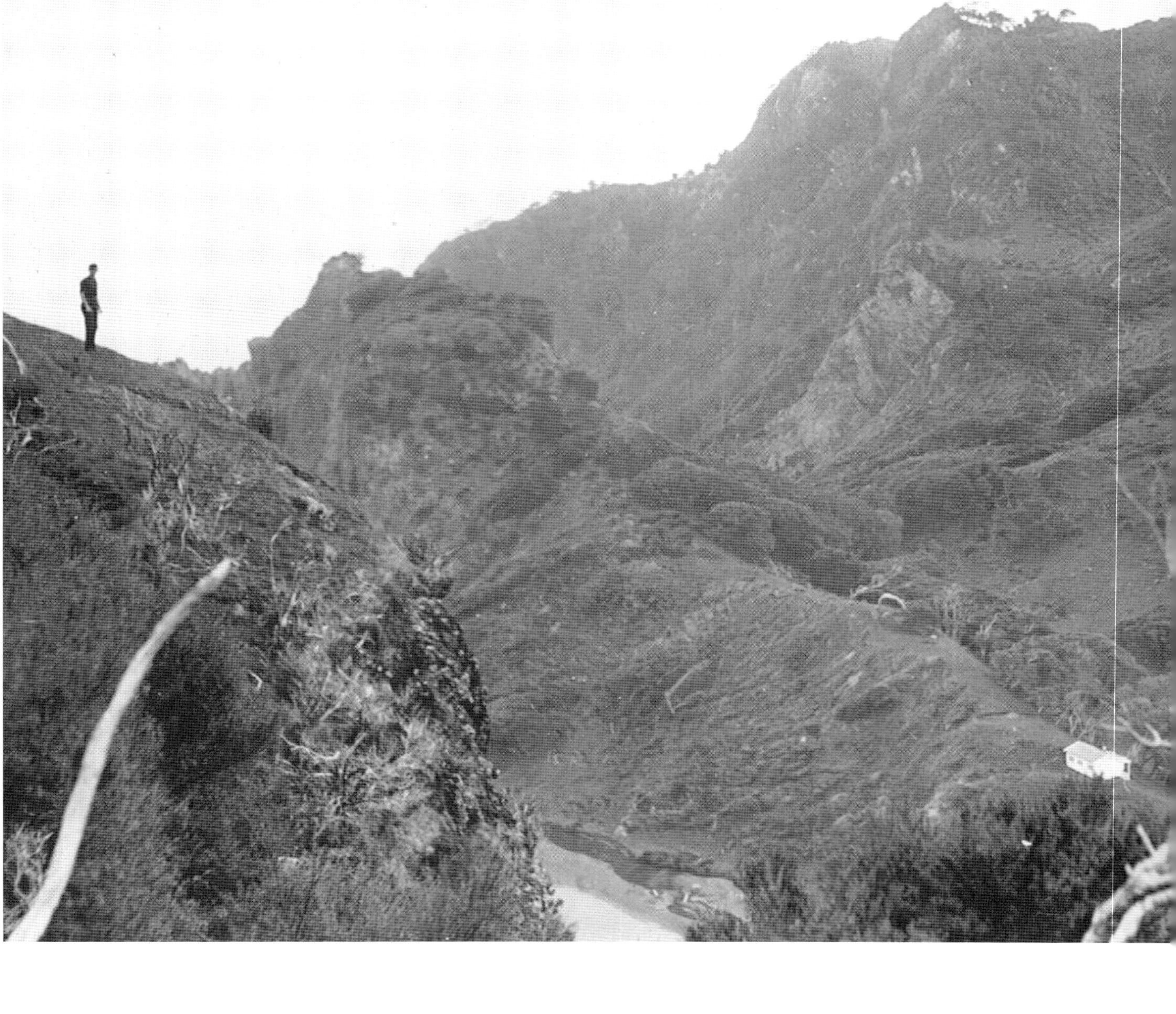

LEFT I stand atop the Big Cone in 1928.

BELOW The two sections on The Watchman bought by Jack Mansell. The cottage on the top section was finished for Mrs Farley in 1928.

FAR BELOW This is the beach house on the Karekare Road, originally owned by Auckland builder, Mr Lyons. Mrs Farley left the house to me after her death on 3 December 1947.

People getting out of their depth with property deals actually happened then as now, and the first to crumble was Jack Mansell with the two on The Watchman. He had actually started to build when the explosion came, and they also came back to Mrs Farley's hands. They say that half a brick is better than none, but half a house is none too good so she had to advertise for a carpenter to come and finish it. This he did and walked all the way out from Glen Eden to look at the job. Plenty of others rang up about it, but this man walked the 15 miles from Glen Eden in a pair of light track shoes; as you can guess, he got the job.

Mr Charlie Hyde

The first two sections on The Watchman were bought by Mr Jack Mansell but, as mentioned above, came back on to Mrs Farley's hands. The name of the carpenter she hired to finish the house was Mr Charlie Hyde. A few days after starting he had all the rafters in place ready to nail and I had gone to get the cows, some of them being on the flat just below him. As I walked among them to go farther in and look for two I could not see, I heard a noise behind me and looked round to see the black heifer Topsy coming straight for me.

What had happened was I had gone between her and her calf, which was asleep under a cutty bush, and not noticed. Being a very good runner I made a dash for the creek and as I reached the bank took a last look before jumping in. As I thought, she had given up and gone back to the calf, but Charlie Hyde, who had seen the whole thing from The Watchman laughed so much that he lost his balance and caught hold of the first rafter, which of course was only sitting there and came out in his hand. He gabbed the next one and so on till he came to the last one and fell in a heap with it in the corner. All this clatter made me look up and it was my turn to laugh as the last rafter with Charlie Hyde embracing it thundered downwards. At dinner that night my mother had heard all about it and asked Charlie if he thought I could run. With a mouthful of potatoes and a few other things he managed to splutter, 'Like a streak of lightening!'

After the cottage was finished, my grandmother got Charlie to put a sitting room on that jutted out from the side of the dining room into the garden. This had an open fireplace and we were to have many comfortable evenings in it in the following winters.

1926

A visitor from the King Country

Just before Easter 1926 we had a chap called Stan Paris come to work for us on the farm. He had a friend working in a timber mill at Pokaka down in the King Country and he came out one day to see his old mate Stan. After having a look around the beach and the Karekare Valley, the man, Mr Ted Norman, said he was sure there were a lot of kauri logs round that could be cut into good timber.

Our powerhouse also impressed him and the circular saw for cutting the firewood. He said this could be easily replaced with a big six-foot one to cut bigger loads of firewood. This was done and a trolley on rails at each end of the bench completed the set up. The next step was to change the pulley around to maximise power; with a full head of water we had about 16 hp.

We now had to get a set of wheels and make a trailer for the Dodge and, as necessity is the mother of invention, this was somehow done. Everything was now ready and a start was made on the logs on the beach first. After they were worked out we started going round Karekare Point to Pararaha on the low tide. To do this it was important to get round Karekare Point as soon as possible so as to have as much time as we could get for loading up before the tide turned. We would go down to the Point early and leave the Dodge high up on the beach with two 12x2 planks from the old tramline under the back wheels. 'The first commandment in beach driving is use planks. The second is you need strength, which the good Lord provided that day. The third, of course, is thou shalt not drive round rocks or through creeks in top gear.

Ted Norman was a big chap, over 6 feet tall and as strong as a bullock. On this day he and I, with my cousin Keith Rule, were on our second trip to Pararaha. After getting loaded up and ready to go we found the crank handle was not in its usual place on the floor by the gear lever. What a situation, the tide was coming in and we realised we must have left it on the ground in the mill yard.

Ted Norman looked at me and then at the fast rising tide. My first thought was to dash back to the mill yard as I was a great runner in those days. The thought was dashed almost at once as I realised good runner that I was, I could not cover the 3½ miles each way and get back in time. I think he guessed my thoughts; he grabbed the timber jack and put the prongs under the body crossarm and jacked up the left back wheel. 'Quick,' he said to me, 'get in and put it in top gear and if she starts keep her going.' He then put both his strong arms over the wheel and spun it over and she started first go. How about that? Imagine his strength, for being in gear he had to turn both the engine and gearbox over by spinning the back wheel. We lost no time in getting away from Pararaha and raced back to the Point with the kauri log behind us. There was no time to spare and as he dropped into second gear for the dash round the Point I was thinking, 'My gosh, that was a near thing for the Dodge again.'

By the end of the winter all the logs had been brought in and cut into planks so Ted Norman left to go back to the King Country. I never saw him again but always remember him as the big chap who worked all through the winter in a black bush singlet. You don't see men like him these days.

My grandfather falls ill

Shortly after the sections were sold my grandfather became ill and had to go into hospital, so we did not have his help that summer. It soon became obvious that he was seriously ill and with the house full of guests for Christmas and not enough umbrellas to keep the road dry, it became somewhat of a job to get to see him. It also became obvious why he had wanted my father to come back to Karekare after we left Stanmore Bay, for he had passed his accountant's exam and he knew he would be able to take over if necessary.

As grandfather's condition got worse and being a Sunday, a few days before Christmas, my mother said we must try and get through to see him. It was decided that Wally Farley, my father, mother and I, in the 1925 Essex would try and get through for visiting hours at 2 o'clock. We left early in the morning with the chains on the back wheels and carried an axe, slash hook, spade and a coil of rope for we knew a real task lay ahead of us.

What I saw that day no-one would believe, least of all the modern motorist. After four hours we had fought our way as far as the Lone Kauri ruts and from there on a car was stuck in every bend right through to

McElwains Flat. In most places you could not get past them so had to get them out first. Dozens of them were trying to get to Piha for Christmas. Just after getting past the Lone Kauri we came on a Model T Ford belonging to the Diamond Taxi Co. The driver had on patent leather shoes and was as much at home in the mud as a polar bear in the desert and the amount of mud around his shoes gave the impression of a skin diver with flippers on. While Wally was telling him that he would never get down to Piha (the hill, by the way, looked like a logging track where bullocks had been dragging logs down for weeks), along came the owner of the Piha boarding house, Mr Ted Legrise, in his big 1925 seven-seater Chandler. These cars were excellent in the mud, some of the best and, like the Essex, came from the United States. I had seen him several times before and knew that he did not like little cars or people who could not drive in the mud and got in his way.

An argument then started between him and the driver of the taxi with his flippers on, soon to be joined by the woman who had hired the taxi. The cause of it was Wally Farley and my father telling her to let Legrise take them on as he knew the road and would get them there. He said he would take them on for a £1 but they had to pay the taxi 25 shillings from town to Piha. This was beyond a joke for the woman in the taxi. She had an advantage over the boys though as there was more at stake, as in the mud, and she could agree with Ted Legrise, Wally Farley, my father and the taxi driver who didn't know which way to turn. Finally Legrise looked at Wally Farley and

The 1927 Essex. My father is at the wheel and about to enter The Devil's Elbow.

said, 'What will I do, run over them?' With his big Chandler turning over he looked quite capable of doing it. After a struggle we got him past and then we got by and they were left robbing the bush of anything that would go under the wheels. Before Legrise left he told us that he had been pulling them out at £1 a time all the way through from Waiatarua. We soon found out as we battled on that he had no sooner pulled them out than they were bogged again.

Finally we got to the bridge in the Nihotupu Valley where we were able to turn round, as the visiting hours had gone, the sun was going and the night was going to be with us soon. It was hard enough having a bad road but to have had drivers heading for a holiday made things really bad. As we fought our way back, there they were all in much the same places, some a few bends further on and others with the front wheels in one rut and the back ones in another, lying right across the road.

At last we got back to Karekare, tired out, covered in mud and having had more than enough for one day. Some of the family got through a few days later and managed to see grandfather for a while. I was 11 and did not get to see him again and as the hospital could do no more for him he was moved to his daughter's place, my Aunt Madge, at Folk Street, New Lynn, where he died on 9 March 1926. I went to the funeral a few days later and he was buried at Waikumete.

Father takes over

My father now had to take over as he had foreseen, and being a busy time for us it was particularly hard on my grandmother, who did a lot of the cooking. Somehow, with much effort, we got through that summer and then another winter was on us. It was now back to the beach again to get all the heavy goods round from Whatipu; things were a bit quicker now as we had bought a half-ton 1922 Dodge truck for the farm and beach. I remember one of these trips very well. We used to take all the empty tins in a box and throw them out at Pararaha. On this particular trip we had a chap with us who was going up to Onehunga on the launch and was all dressed for town. As we got to Pararaha, Wally Farley, who was driving, called out, 'Throw the tins out,' and this chap who was sitting at the back of the truck called out, 'I will.' With that he stood up with them but lost his balance and went with them into the creek. We all laughed so much that we had gone about a mile before any of us could make Wally understand that his passenger had bailed out without a parachute.

We got through the winter of 1926 with events like this to laugh at. One

John, Dudley and myself, 1926.

MY THREE SONS

day my mother and I had gone to town for some reason and were to come back the next day with Ted Legrise's brother, Laurie, who was a taxi driver and lived in Balmoral Road. When we got to his place Ted Legrise was also going to come back and he took the wheel of his brother's seven-seater Chandler and drove us to Glen Eden in seven minutes. This was the fastest trip I had ever had and was more than enough for Mrs Laurie Legrise who made him hand over the wheel to her husband then and there. Just think of it, Balmoral Road to Glen Eden in seven minutes in those days. As we came over the hill to go down to Avondale we were nearly airborne.

This was no laughing matter, as you will see. One day the road had dried out a bit so Wally Farley, my father and I set off for Glen Eden to get the mail and some other goods. On the way back we had just come down Darkey's Hill and got up the next rise on to Byles Flat when we saw a pair of eyes, caught in the headlights, looking at us from the water table. I could see that it was a big black bull and Wally Farley turned the lights off and said to keep quite still and he might go off into the bush, which he did after a while. If we had been stupid enough to try and drive past he would probably have charged the car, but our bush sense told us what to do. This was the last wild bull that I saw as there were not many wild cattle left in the Waitakere Ranges now. So I can say that 1926 just about saw the last of the descendants of the wreck of the *Orwell*.

On 19 April my sister, Eileen, was born, just 41 days after my grandfather died. I can remember staying with my Aunt Madge for a few days and going on the bus to Avondale, I then changed to the tram for the rest of the way to see her. When mother arrived home with Eileen it was not on a sledge like John had arrived on at Stanmore Bay, there was a rough road but no rough water before the sledge ride.

Kids aboard the 1927 Essex 4. On the right is my sister Eileen, born 19 April 1926.

From left: Laurie Farley, my sister-in-law Jessie, John Badham, myself and Pat McPhillips, 1938. I'm getting ready to attack the chop suey. This is the only picture I have of Pat McPhillips.

As the summer of 1926 approached I was going to be 12. We have yet another Essex, a 1926 model, and hired a 1926 seven-seater Hudson from Dominion Motors for the Christmas rush. We also had another man come to work for us and his name was Pat McPhillips from Belfast, Ireland. He had been a stroker in the Olympics during World War I. He was a hardy man and if ever my grandmother was going to make a batch of scones she would say, 'Pat, get me a nice hot fire,' which paid havoc to the ti-tree to the tune of a ton a day.

I did both standards four and five this year, along with my cousin Kathleen, so when school started again in February 1927 we went to standard six. My main job all through that winter of 1926 was getting the cows and helping with the firewood that my grandmother and Pat knew how to burn so well.

My sister Eileen was eight months old while the rush was on and my mother, apart from her work, had to attend to her as well. My brother Dudley was given the job of taking her out in the pram while John followed at a safe distance with his cart.

1927

Early in 1927 my Aunt Madge became ill and she came out to stay for a while as they all thought the change would do her good. I remember one day how she came up on The Point with me to get the cows and as it was a very hot we sat down for a while in the shade of a flax bush. While resting we talked about the days at Stanmore Bay and she then told me more about what it was like when they first came to Karekare in 1900.

I don't know what her illness was but she seemed to be mentally upset at times as though she was worrying about something. After a while she went back to New Lynn and my mother looked after her two boys, Keith and Ron, who went to school with us all through 1927. Keith was just three weeks younger than me, being born on 5 January 1915.

Stuck in the sand

One morning my father and Wally Farley set off early to go to Whatipu with the Dodge truck to get some supplies. When they got to Karekare Point they stopped and my father got out to go and have a look from the rocks when the waves went back, to see if it was all right for them to come on. This was always done as a precaution because the beach was always changing due to the movement of the Manukau Bar. For some reason Wally Farley did not wait for the signal to come on, but started to go as soon as the waves went back and right in front of the Point went into a crab hole, as we used to call them, and the motor cut out. The hole was about three feet deep and of course water got into the distributor, but that was not the worst part for they soon found out that they had made a mistake with the tide and it was coming in, not going out.

Somehow word reached the house that the Dodge was stuck in the tide and it was coming in. A mad rush started for the beach and I can remember very well how my cousin Ron leapt out of bed and in his haste put both legs into the same leg of his trousers, doing a spectacular reel before crashing in the corner. I dashed off to get Molly and was in such a hurry that I did not have time to laugh. Having got Molly and with a collar, hammer, chains and holding the swindle-tree [part of the harness between the horse and a cart or wagon] in front of me, set off at a gallop for The Point. All across the bay people were running along the soft sand as I passed them. When I got to The Point the tide was well around the car and Wally Farley was about to wade out to rescue his dog Paddy, who was still in the front seat. We got Molly hitched on but she was frightened of the waves coming in and after the third attempt the rope from the Dodge to the swindle-tree broke and Molly cleared out across the soft sand, dragging the chains and with me in hot pursuit.

I could not catch up to her in the soft sand so decided to go at a 40° angle for about 30 yards until I was in front of her and then turn in to try and leap on to her back. I was about to start the run in when I saw the lawyer, Jack Mansell, coming down by The Watchman with his Hudson, so I turned and went back to the Point.

He got there before I did and had two long ropes that had been joined together. My father and Wally were up to their waists in water as they got the end tied to the Dodge. Mansell kept saying to me as I came up to the Hudson, 'We will soon have her out,' but we all made the mistake of not putting solid planks under the back wheels before starting the pull. As soon

The soft sand that I had to gallop through the morning the Dodge became submerged.

as the Hudson got the strain, down went the back wheels in the sand and the rope had to be let go as everyone struggled to save the Hudson from the fast rising tide.

After a long battle we got it, inch by inch, up to high watermark where it had to be left until the tide went out. It was all wet inside and the saltwater damage amounted to £150. As for the Dodge, it was six hours under the tide and we all had to pull it out with the horses at low tide and bring it back to the house. The front seat came up on Muriwai Beach several days later, as the current flows north.

Two mechanics then came out from Northern Automobiles, the Dodge agents, and they stripped it all down, washed everything in kerosene then put it all back, and gave her a swing on the crank handle and away she went. So after six hours under the tide she started first pop and did thousands more miles round the farm and beach before the salt air and sand laid her to rest. Not bad for a 1922 model. This is the one I learned to drive in and she was still running on the beach in 1932; when I left Karekare in 1950 what I didn't know about driving on a beach wasn't worth knowing.

Not so long after this event a racing car came out one day for practice runs on the beach at low tide. The driver was Wizard Smith who raced a lot at Muriwai and I think also the 90 Mile Beach. He gave me and my cousin Kathleen a ride in it to Pararaha and back a few times at speeds between 70–75 miles an hour, which was fast in those days. Each time he flashed past the Point I thought of the Dodge and the lesson we learned that morning.

The big flood — Christmas 1927

Winchelsea House, as usual, was booked out for Christmas and on the evening of 23 December there was very heavy rain, which continued all night and much more must have come down up the hill. At 2 a.m. it was at its height and most of us were up by then and could hear the roar of water everywhere. It was pitch dark with the water all over the veranda and lapping the top of the doorstep, when with a roar it suddenly started to recede; it was frightening because you could not see what was happening.

Wally Farley was up on the Clear Hill with a lantern calling out at this time and he yelled out, 'I think the bridge has gone.' Indeed it had. What had happened was the bridge had formed a dam from bits of logs and tree heads left behind in the bush from the timber mill days. These had been swept down in to the torrent and jammed under the bridge, forming a dam. Eventually the pressure of the water had torn the bridge out. Away went everything, the bridge hit the old tramline and tore the dance hall off its

The creek in flood, 1904.

blocks, swinging one end round about 30°. The bridge and tramlines swept on down the beach and ended up where the tramline crossed the creek in front of The Watchman. If the bridge had not gone when it did the water would have been coming down the passage in to the drawing room. I have thought over the years what a frightful sight it would have been had it been daylight. It would have terrified the guests.

Wally Farley and his family were in the cottage by the powerhouse. To the side is a watercourse and creek, which comes from the back of the Clear Hill. The overflow from the pelton wheel also goes into the creek, which runs past the cottage. A few days before some of the men had been up this watercourse throwing ti-tree down for firewood; this formed another dam that sent the water into the cottage. My cousin Kathleen could hear the dogs yelping in the porch and got up to see what the trouble was. As she opened the door they floated in sitting on boxes that had been going round and round in the porch.

The clean-up job in the morning was the worst, with logs and mud covering the lawn and looking like the Devil's parlour. As the bridge had gone, the seven-seater Hudson was stranded on the wrong side, so after the creek had gone down and the sand hardened it had to be driven over The Watchman and down behind the dance hall then across the creek on to the sand and back up to the powerhouse.

The Karekare Cutting was blocked by two big slips and the guests that could be reached by phone or telegram before they left home were told to go out to Onehunga Wharf and get the launch down to Whatipu. From there Harry Gibbons brought them along the beach in his old truck to Karekare Point and we met them and carried all the bags over the rocks to the Dodge truck on the other side. The worst slip on The Cutting was just above the bend we called Totevirbus and took several days to clear. In the meantime all the supplies had to be brought in a car from Glen Eden and carried over the slip and put on a sledge for the trip down to the house.

The waterfall in flood, 1904.

The waterfall in flood, 1922.

As the flume at the head of the waterfall had also been washed away, we had no electric light for several days and no circular saw to cut the kitchen firewood. It was hard work from daylight till dark and did seem like hell with the high water gone. Somehow we got through it all and we learned later that the beach store at Muriwai had been taken off its blocks and went out to sea.

We had to order a new flume, which was shipped to Onehunga then came down the Manukau by launch to Whatipu. This flume was 12x12 galvanised iron and looked like spouting from Jack the giant killer's house. The men on the wharf at Onehunga and the launch could not make out what this big spouting was for and thought we must be expecting monsoons.

Our little dance hall had to be jacked up and reblocked in its new position. Bottle-jacks were used to lift it up. The hall continued into the 1960s as a local community centre, great for dances and surf club parties. It's a private house with many additions.

Before closing the chapter on 1927, I shall say that I obtained my Standard Seven proficiency on 30 November 1927, along with Kathleen Farley and Keith Rule. I then did all of 1928 on secondary under Mr T.U. Wells while Kathleen Farley went to Auckland Girls Grammar and my mate Keith Rule started work with Motor Specialists in Anzac Avenue in Auckland City.

1928

A decision had been taken to put an asphalt tennis court up on The Watchman just below Mrs Farley's cottage. As it was Depression times and jobs were scarce as hens' teeth, Charlie Hyde wanted to stay on and help with it. The job was undertaken by a Mr Tanner who had three men with him.

All the cement for the tennis court job had to come down from Onehunga to Whatipu and then along the beach in the Dodge truck that had been six hours under the tide. My father and Charlie Hyde did this job as well as cart 72 yards of shingle and rock from the creek. The embankment end below the cottage was a terrace of stone to seat 60 people, who had a fine view of the game.

Those coming for the Christmas holidays that summer of 1928 were pleasantly surprised and amazed that the job had all been done in less than three weeks. It was a favourite place after dinner at night and many excellent games I have had there.

On the tennis court, 1941. Left to right: (unknown), Eileen Badham, Betty Banks and Wally Badham.

The disappearance of Mr Stanhold

After Easter of 1928 a guest at the house, Mr Stanhold, had decided to stay on through the winter. He was a peculiar sort of chap and was always moaning about himself.

One Sunday, about the middle of the winter, there was a westerly gale blowing with a big sea running as well. Mr Stanhold was in the habit of going for walks and on this day was seen going down the beach with a blanket, but no-one thought anything of it at the time. When it came to lunch there was no sign of him so several of us set out to look around. I made for the fishing rocks and the base of the cliff between there and The Watchman, but could find no tracks. My father with Mr Ted Browne

Mr Trevor Lloyd visits

I began the following year as a guide for Mr Trevor Lloyd, who was cartoonist for the *New Zealand Herald*. He was a regular guest and as he had made a study of the early Maoris, was keen on looking for lost curios. My father arranged for me to take him round to Pararaha and show him all the caves and likely spots. The first one I made for was under Mt Zion and you had to go down on hands and knees to start the way in. I do not like caves and was not going to go in so said I would wait outside for him. He had two torches with him and was soon out of sight so I began the wait and wondered how long he would be gone. After about an hour and no sight or sound from him, I was getting a bit anxious and wondering what to do, when along came two men. I told them Mr Lloyd had gone in the cave, but I did not like the look of them and manoeuvred quietly so as not to be trapped in the entrance. While we were talking, much to my relief, Lloyd appeared and said he had found nothing. It had been cleaned out.

We then started off for the Pararaha, following the cliffs round and through the old tunnel where the engine used to run. I cut round the edge of the swamp and into the Pararaha Gorge. There are some small caves on the headland but they are not easy to get at so we headed up the gorge a bit and then crossed over and came back on the other side. It was here that he had his first find, a stone axe, lying on a patch of bare ground. I don't know how he spotted it before me as I had very sharp eyes in those days, but think it was because I was on the lookout for any movement of any kind. That was the only find of the day, though we looked in many other likely spots. A look at the sun told me it was time to start for home as we had to go back up the gorge to cross over and then get back round The Point before the tide got too high. We arrived home and Mr Lloyd said he had enjoyed the day and although he had found the axe, would not have done so without his guide.

A few days later he was digging in the big cave above the Cascades and found a lump of greenstone as big as your head. He had it all worked out as to how it got there, telling me the old Maoris had hidden it.

Above Mt Zion. The first cave I took Mr Lloyd to is just to the left of the dark clump of pohutakawa trees.

Left Pararaha Gorge.

went round the Point to Pararaha and could find no tracks or sign of him either, so went all the way to Whatipu. It was then thought that he must have got washed off the rocks and nothing was found for a week.

The following Sunday some men had gone down to Whatipu and while walking along the beach at Windy Point saw footmarks going into the big caves and none coming out. They thought this was strange and decided to go and have a look and see what was going on. The riddle was soon solved for as far in as it was possible to get was a dead man wrapped up in a blanket. Mr Stanhold it was and he had taken his life with poison. The bits of the jigsaw puzzle were now easily put together. He left no tracks because he walked along the edge of the tide and then up the Pararaha Creek. We think he then got out of sight. He would be sure to see my father and Mr Browne and maybe waited for them to come back from Whatipu. What a tragedy; we talked about Mr Stanhold for weeks.

View from the Fishing Rocks in 1904.

My father's first car — 1924 Essex 4

My father had now bought his first car, a 1924 Essex 4, from Mr Hugo Cooper, who was workshop foreman at Northern Automobiles at the time and used to come out to the coast quite a bit. The price was £95, quite a lot of money then.

The car, with its big 4-cylinder engine and high gear, was rated the best hill climber in America. It could do 45 mph in second and with the traditional crash box of this bygone era, would be more than a match for any of today's drivers.

When my father took his first trip down the Cutting with it (all clay then), he had to put it in low gear and steer like hell round the corners; he dared not touch the brake or he would have ended up in the Cutting Creek 200 feet below. By the time he got to the bottom of Slippery Rock it was doing a screaming 25 mph in low gear.

The Essex 4 on the old clay road surrounded by some lovely bush.

The car was originally owned by a Mr Collecutt who was a stockcar racer at Muriwai with it in 1924, doing over 75 mph. This was fast for an ordinary car then.

It had several appreciable features such as shutters in front of the radiators, an oil gauge, a thermometer on the radiator cap and an air brake cooling device that let cold air into the cylinder with a whistling sound while going down a hill. This was used if the temperature was up after climbing the Waitakere Ranges to Waiatarua on a hot day. Care had to be taken not to leave it on for long as it would cool the engine right down.

A peculiar feature was that the front wheels were held on by a centre thread, like a nut screws on to a bolt. This fitting was made of brass and the thread got worn and gave my father a bit of trouble the following year. It was this trouble that caused him to trade it on a 1927 Essex in May 1930.

I never got a chance to drive this car as I did not start driving till the winter of 1930, and that was with the 1922 Dodge on the farm and beach between Karekare and Whatipu. I got my licence in October 1930 with the 1927 Essex and gave a lot of help with the driving that summer.

Leaving home

With the Depression on it did not seem much good going on with more secondary education, so I decided to call it a day and learn something I had become interested in: beekeeping. The place was Pearson's in Hamilton, known as Pearson Bees of East Street, who had over 1200 hives and wanted a boy to work through the season.

My father decided to take me in the Essex 4 and my brothers, Dudley and John, came along for the ride. We left early in the morning and got to Hamilton just before lunch as it was a very different road then, nearly all metal chip with no easy Bombay Hill like now. You had to go over the Razor Back, which terrorised some city motorists but was nothing to us after the Karekare Cutting.

With me settled in and after a bit of lunch they set out on the return trip and I was to learn later that they had quite a bit of trouble on the way back. If you remember, I said the front wheels were held on by a centre thread that had become worn and was to give my father a lot of trouble. Well this was it and although I can't remember just where as I was not there, one of the front wheels came off and rolled across the road. Fortunately they were not going fast and were able to pull up. They got the wheel and wrapped a bit of twine over the thread then put it on and started off again.

I settled down after a few days but found it a different environment to what I was used to. The apiaries were situated all round Hamilton and they had some at Waitakaruru on the Hauraki Plains. The brother that I was staying with, Tom Pearson, worked the Waitakaruru apiaries with a man to help him and the other brother, Alby, and I did the Hamilton ones.

I got stung quite a bit to start with but soon got used to them and they did not bother me then. We took off 40 tons of honey that year and the two of us would do a ton a day with Alby on the uncapping and me working the 4-frame reversible extractor. While we were working and driving out to the apiaries I used to tell him all about Karekare and when Easter was coming up he said he and his wife and little boy would like to come and stay a few days. I came with them and my father met us at the Auckland Railway Station. They liked the drive out and thought the place was great, also the tennis court, which was getting a lot of use.

With Easter over they left to go back and said I could stay a few more days. My father was taking them back to the train and was going down Forest Hill Road to give them a different view when just before the corner that turns off to go back to the West Coast Road the front wheel came off again. After getting it back on he had to go slow to the Glen Eden station and put them on the train there.

I went back on my own a few days later on the Rotorua Express, driven by my old friend who gave me the ride in Sandfly at Karekare 12 years earlier, Jack Sergeant. I got off at Frankton Junction and got a bus over to Hamilton. In those days you had to share the bridge over

This strange tree, burnt and dead, guarded a section of the West Coast Road (now Piha Road) to the coast for many years.

the Waikato River with the train. If you got caught in the middle and didn't like clouds of steam on you, too bad.

I worked all the winter with them and learned comb-foundation making as well. Other beekeepers used to send their beeswax to them and we would make it into comb-foundation and return it to them. It was quite interesting work and except for the melting of the wax, was an indoor job.

I remember one day we were at one of the apiaries that was near the Waikato River and we had gone down to have our lunch on the riverbank. Alby's father-in-law was with us and we had all finished our lunch and gone down to the edge of the water. There was about a six-foot strip from the bank to the edge of the water that you could stand on and we were all having a look round before going back to work.

Suddenly, round the corner came a paddle-steamer with a huge paddle in the stern; I sized the situation up promptly and started getting back up the bank. The other two were so interested in watching the speed that she was going down the river that they did not realise what was coming. I had not had a good laugh all day so pretended to be packing things up while I waited for the big wave from the stern to strike each bank. The next thing was a yell; I had a hard job to keep a straight face as I looked down and saw them up to their waists in water, grabbing at branches of willow trees.

I left them at the end of September and took another job with Mr W.P. Clark of Matatoki, seven miles from Thames. My father and mother came down and took me there through Te Aroha, and we had a swim in the baths before going on.

I was not yet 15 and was to look after 100 hives of bees and help Mr Clark and another boy of 19 to milk 75 cows night and morning. I was only there a month as I went down with the flu and was three days in bed, so my father and mother came down and brought me back to Karekare.

The trip back from Thames across the Hauraki Plains was a very different road then to what it is now. Of course we had to climb the Razor Back but fortunately the wheel did not come off. Back to Karekare on 15 November 1929. I was to pick up my stockwhip and start where I had left off. I was 15 on 11 December and helped my parents over Christmas and New Year.

1930

In early January 1930 I smelt the honey again and left to work the season for Mr R. Stewart of Amahou Street, Rotorua. My father took me down to the Auckland Railway Station and saw me off on the Rotorua Express. Even now, after all these years, I can still remember his last word of advice, 'When you get off at Rotorua just stand to one side and he will come up to you.'

Mr Stewart did just that. We went over to his car, the latest model Chrysler 75, painted a beautiful maroon. In a few minutes we were at his home in Amahou Street, just behind Brents, and I was introduced to his wife.

I soon settled down as I liked Rotorua and he had much better equipment than Pearson Brothers. A boiler to provide steam for the uncapping knife and a Benton capping melter and honey pump that would pump to a height of 12 feet and round a right angle. Also, the latest eight-frame reversible extractor with a fast and loose pulley for working the honey pump.

The next day we ran into a bit of trouble when we pulled the honey pump down to clean it. It worked on the same principle as the pump on a Dodge car, which was eccentric and had eight screws that would fit back in any position but would only work in one position. For some strange reason the makers had not shown which was the correct position. Perhaps they had struck the same trouble while testing it and were so worn out that they forgot to mark the place. After hours of trying to puzzle it out Mr Stewart went and got the borough engineer to come and have a look. He was stumped for a while till he suddenly got an idea and said to make a mark at the first place and then keep turning it round one screw at a time and see what happens. After the fifth move we struck the right spot.

With that problem over we got started on extracting the honey, going out each morning in the truck to one of the apiaries at a time and bringing the heavy supers back to the shed beside the house. After lunch, with Mr Stewart doing the uncapping and me working the extractor, we would have a ton off by 5 p.m. As soon as the honey was up to the bottom bars of the extractor I would slide the belt for the honey pump on to the loose pulley and it would pump up, over my head, and into a ton tank behind me.

Each morning after breakfast we would take the Benton capping melter and wash it in a hot pool in the ti-tree scrub behind the town. Although there was plenty of steam all round we did not see anyone having a sauna. By the end of February we had worked out the Rotorua apiaries and started to get ready to go to the Bay of Plenty for six weeks. We camped by the honeyshed at the end of Cameron Road, Te Puke.

We left one morning with the truck and our gear and a lovely drive it was, past Okere Falls, the edge of Lake Rotoiti then over Wairakarata to Te Puke. Then, on to Papamoa for the night and slept in the honey-shed that night as this was to be the first apiary to start on. Papamoa is between Mt Maunganui and Maketu and it was at Maketu that the canoes Arawa and Tainui are said to have landed from the great migration of 1350 AD.

The next morning Mr Stewart got the service car back to Rotorua so he could bring his wife and the Chrysler down. I started clearing the grass from round the hives while he was away and getting things ready for the next day. Late in the afternoon he arrived and he put up a tent for me to sleep in and a place to have our meals. They slept in the car as the front seat folded back to make a bed.

After working Papamoa out we moved to Te Puke and camped by the honeyshed as I said before, in Cameron Road. Each morning we went out to the apiaries that were all round Paengaroa and brought the honey back to Te Puke. In the afternoon we did the extracting and I have never seen hives so high as those Paengaroa apiaries. I had to stand in the back of the truck to prise the lids off them. Twenty super high hives and all 12-frame, propped up with iron frames so they wouldn't fall over.

Each Sunday we used to go to the beach for the day, either Mount Maunganui or Maketu. We liked the Mount. Even back then the Mount was crowded. Every weekend it would be like Blackpool on a bank holiday with a free beer thrown in.

The work went steadily on and soon we had got to the last apiary, which took us into early April. This is the worst time to be working an apiary as the honey flow is over and all worker bees are home. Care must be taken not to have a hive open for long as the sight of honey will start trouble and you can get stung to ribbons. At this time I have had as many as 20 stings between the wrist and elbow in less than 10 minutes but took no notice, but just kept getting the supers into the truck and covered as quickly as possible. The stings had no effect on me and my arms didn't swell. On the last day the bees got so agitated we had to light a fire and let plenty of smoke drift through the apiary. Imagine an apiary of 50, all 20 supers high, well over 100,000 bees in each hive, ready to pounce on an open hive.

An incident happened at one of the Paengaroa apiaries one morning. It was our practice to put escape boards on the hives in the afternoon that we were going to work on the next day. The boards were placed just below the last super we intended to take off. They allowed all the bees in the top supers to come down at night but they couldn't get back up. A lot of time was saved the next morning if we could back up the truck and just lift all these supers, which were free of bees, straight into the truck.

On this particular morning some local Maoris had seen us back the truck up and came over on their bikes to the edge of the fence to watch us get the honey off. Now, we did not want them to know that the top supers down to the second one had no bees in them, because the temptation was too great. Stewart gave me a wink and I knew what to do. So we went behind the first big hive and brought the heel of my boot hard against the bottom super. With us out of the way behind the hives, the bees shot out and took to them in a swarm and got rid of unwanted visitors. We both had a good laugh as we watched the speed of those bikes, with them pedalling so hard the back wheels were leaping off the ground.

As summer turned to autumn in 1930 we packed up. I enjoyed my six weeks in the Bay of Plenty. I was glad to have a few more days in Rotorua before I would return to my beloved Karekare for the winter.

Flying

The next day, 18 April, was to be a notable one for me. Captain M.C. McGregor, DFC, of Hamilton Airways, whom I had seen flying out of a paddock at Te Rapa while with Pearson Brothers, had now flown a Gipsy Moth ZK-AAV down to Rotorua for Easter of 1930.

Captain Malcolm Charles McGregor was a World War I pilot who flew with the squadron commanded by the famous Canadian, Major 'Billy' Bishop, and known on the Western Front as 'Bishop Circus'. While in the government grounds with Mr Stewart, we saw him arrive and circle the town before going to land on the old aerodrome, which was down Whaka Road on the left-hand side. I said I would like to go up for a flight, so after lunch we drove down in the Chrysler and I went over to Mrs McGregor, who was booking the flights, and asked for a stunting flight. She said so many people had asked for them and been sick that her husband decided to put the price up to £1 10 shillings; she would have a word with him if I waited around for a few minutes. I got a flight straight away.

Mrs McGregor gave me a helmet and goggles and I got up on the wing and into the cockpit of ZK-AAV. Mr McGregor showed me how to fasten the belt. The wind was from the east, which meant taking off over the lake and coming into the land over Whakarere. Mr and Mrs Stewart watched as we taxied out towards Whakarere and then turned in to the wind. The ground seemed to rush past with terrific speed and the next thing we were out over the lake. He flew all over the lakes and the town and then back round Mt Ngongotaha. As we came back over Whaka at 3,000 feet he asked, 'Would you like a loop? My wife asked me to give you one without the extra charge.' I replied, 'I would love to stunt up here with such a famous pilot.' The next thing the nose went down, the ground vanished and my legs were above my head, so we were upside-down over Whaka.

We came out in a steep dive and there was the ground below again. I could see all the cars on the edge of the aerodrome. I thought I could just about see Mr and Mrs Stewart holding their breath. Then a nice glide in through the steam from the hotpools coming up at us. The ground got closer and then a smooth landing, one of the thousands that he made. I thanked him for the thrilling ride before going over to tell the Stewarts all about it. Little did I realise then that just 18 months later I would be a pilot myself and one of the planes I would be flying was a Tiger Moth imported from Australia.

A day after I had my flight a home-made plane was flown over from Whakatane and McGregor went out to escort him in. Everyone was looking at this plane as it circled the lake and aerodrome, even now I can still see it as it just fell out of the sky from about 60 feet after passing over Whaka and right on the edge of the aerodrome. Of course I did not know then what the cause of it was, but after I started flying I soon knew that the pilot had come in too slow and she stalled about 60 feet from the ground. He was not hurt, just a few cuts and scratches and shock. I ran over and helped to get him out. The plane was a total mess, but still we admired him, a real plucky chap to fly over all that rough country between Whakatane and Rotorua in a home-made plane.

I return home

The next morning I went to the Rotorua Post Office and booked a call for Karekare. My mother answered the phone and I told here I was leaving the next day at 10 a.m. and would arrive in Auckland at 4 p.m. I then told her that I had been up in an aeroplane all round Rotorua with former stunt Captain McGregor and that he had given me a loop over Whaka. The next day my father met me at the Auckland Railway Station (which was behind the Chief Post Office then) with the Essex 4. On 20 April 1930 I was once again heading back to Karekare.

Winchelsea House, Karekare, 20 April 1930.

A stay in hospital

About the middle of June I got a cut on my left hand that went septic. My father and mother took me to Dr Pettit at Mt Albert and he said I had an abscess under my arm and would have to go into hospital. He also said I was just at the age where if I had been a bit younger or older it would probably not have happened.

So into the children's ward of Auckland Hospital. I went there for six weeks. I had an awful night the night before they operated, my shoulder

Betty Atkins and the bull

Easter was over with, and the crowd had all gone. Betty Atkins had come to work over Easter as a waitress and was staying on for a while. A few days later she wanted to go round to the Pararaha Valley as some of the guests had been there over Easter and told her how spectacular and beautiful it was. My mother said that I could take her as she did not want to go alone.

We took some lunch and left the next morning, crossing the gap on the Point as the sun came up to get the maximum time on the other side while the tide was running out. After getting her over the rocks when the surf was low, I turned in at Mt Zion and followed the cliffs round to the tunnel. She wouldn't believe me when I said we were going through a tunnel where the engine used to run taking the truck loads of timber to Whatipu.

She looked at it as we went through and on the other side said, 'Goodness, Wally, however did they get through all that rock and when did the engine last run?' I told her it was 1918 and that I had a ride in the cab of the engine called Sandfly.

We continued on and we went round the edge of the swamp and then up on the top of the big sandhill, then headed into the mouth of the gorge. She thought it delightful as we worked our way up the creek to a spot known as the old picnic ground. After lunch we went on farther up till we reached a spot where I said it was not advisable to go on and also the position of the sun told me it was time to retrace our steps. All went well till we got to the mouth of the gorge and I was setting the pace about 40 yards ahead, as I was thinking of the gap at Karekare Point that we had to cross before the tide got too high.

Standing in the creek was a shorthorn wild bull and I had gone past thinking she would follow behind. Betty was terrified and refused to come. I had to go back and get between her and the bull. To be honest, I was getting a bit impatient now as the bull was as quiet as an old dairy cow and besides we had three miles to go to reach the Point. Betty was frozen with fear. After a few more stern words I grabbed hold of her and said, 'Come on, we can't waste any more time. You will have to walk a lot faster now or we will end up spending the night in the dark, damp tunnel.' That did it. We reached the Point and after I had got her across the gap I said to her, 'Okay, you can have a rest now. It's only half an hour to the house.' Back at the house she had to tell my mother all about how the bull didn't seem to mind me at all but was watching her all the time ready to charge. My mother stood up for me and told her if it had been a wild bull I would not have taken her near it so she had no need to be afraid.

The picnic ground is just to the right, bottom corner. We had our lunch by this pool.

The Iron-Bound Coast

throbbed and I could not sleep and must have been groaning when the night nurse came and asked what the matter was.' I told her how my arm hurt and she gave me something and said I would be better in the morning. About 7 a.m. I was taken out of the ward as they decided to operate and when I came awake I was on a stretcher and about to be carried back to the ward. I felt so much better. I said to the sister, 'I am okay now, I will walk back to the ward.' She put her hand on me and said, 'You stay there, you will do no such thing.' Back in the ward they all wanted to know how I was and I said, 'I am fine, thank you. I wanted to walk back but they wouldn't let me.' The nurse who had looked after me when I came in was the first to come and see me when she heard I was back. After all these years I can still remember her name, Nurse Tulley; she had dark hair and eyes and was very good to me in the six weeks I was there.

You will probably wonder why I was six weeks. I had a rubber tube under my arm to drain it away and it all healed up too soon and had to be opened up again. This was done by three nurses sitting on me so I couldn't move and a sister opening it up with a probe, a thing with a handle like a spoon. Gosh it hurt and weak as I was it took all three of them to hold me down. I told Nurse Tulley about it when she came on in the afternoon and she said, 'Oh Wally, they are hard aren't they? Never mind, it is over now and I will get you something nice for your tea.' She told me later that when I was in the operating theatre the amount of pus that came away would have filled a pudding basin.

This setback kept me twice as long as it should have done and when they took the tube out it was clean and left me with only a stiff arm. The sister said I must work my arm up and down to get it right or I would lose the use of it. Nurse Tulley used to say, 'Come on Wally, you must get it right up, I know it hurts but I will help you.' Gradually it got right and it was time for me to leave. I often wonder what happened to Nurse Tulley.

Learning to drive

My father and mother came with the Essex 4 to take me home, so once again back to Karekare about the end of July. The next thing was to learn to drive, so my father started me on the Dodge truck when getting firewood and soon I was driving on the beach between Karekare and Whatipu. The next step was to go on to the 1925 Essex.

I soon settled down to the farm work with my uncle, Wally Farley. My grandmother gave me a hive of bees which was to come from Paltridge Apiary and north of Matamata.

The 1927 Essex outside the old garage below the tennis court.

The flat ground in front of the sand hill, summer 1930.

My father and I set off in the Essex 4 to go to Glen Eden for the mail and supplies. Just after we passed Harnetts store on the junction of West Coast Road and Forest Hill Road, the left front wheel came off again and trundled across the road, right in front of Charlie Martin, who was coming towards us from his garage at Glen Eden. I can still see the bewildered look on his face as it bounced like a kangaroo across the road in front of him and jumped the fence in to the paddock. If he had been going a bit quicker or it had come off a split second later he would have been clean bowled and all out. I got over the fence and went after the wheel. The axle had ploughed a strip along the road, which was metal chip, for about 15 feet. We got the wheel on and put some twine round the thread to help to hold it on and crept to Glen Eden. We got back home driving very slowly and my father decided he would trade it in with Dominion Motors on the advice of Mr Mart Donnelly, a friend who was in charge of spare parts and often came out to Karekare. The car he recommended was a 1927 Essex, which was also a tourer with side curtains.

I now started driving the 1927 Essex and was getting quite good with all three, the 1922 Dodge, the 1925 Essex and the 1927 Essex. In October my father thought it was time for me to go for my licence and I remember that day very well. The traffic officer sat in front with me and in the back was my father, mother and grandmother who had come along for the ride. It was the 1927 Essex and I passed the test with ease.

With Christmas 1930 now only a few days away it was decided that I should go to Glen Eden with the 1925 Essex and bring back all the bread, meat and mail. I would then do a second trip and bring back any luggage that my father, Wally Farley and Mart Donnelly could not cope with. The suitcases were all placed on the running board and tied on with rope and the driver would climb over his door to get in. With no passengers I had both sides full with suitcases and got in and out over the door.

Through that summer my cousin, Woee Farley, worked the farm with me getting the cows, milking, fencing, looking after the electric light plant and flume, and of course the firewood, which required a ton a day.

1931

With New Year's Eve over we were now into 1931. January was always a busy month with between 30-40 in the house so I was everywhere; in the kitchen, the stockyard, along the flume, in the bush, on the road, down the beach with the Dodge or looking for a missing cow and, on occasion, some missing guests who were stranded in the swamp at Pararaha. Tracking the cattle and horses is one thing but tracking people is another.

Betty Atkins came back for the season with a girlfriend, Kathleen Tui. I said for fun that when the crowd left I would take both round to Pararaha. Kath looked at me and commented she had heard all about that bull and the tunnel. They were both very efficient in the dining room and popular with the guests, some of whom liked to come and congratulate the kitchen staff also on the speed with which the meals were served; sixty all through in an hour, washing up done and the staff all sitting down to their meal.

Widening The Cutting

The Waitemata Council had decided to widen The Cutting and also provide work for a lot of men. These were public works men and it was the Depression period of the 1930s. This would mean that the hill would be a lot worse for a while than it already was. So with these gangs working and the clay dropping off the wheelbarrows as they went to the edge to dump it, you can imagine what it was like after only a shower of rain. All these men went home for the weekend and we had to take them to Glen Eden every Friday night and bring them back on Sunday night. As the winter came on the road was a frightful mess, not only The Cutting but all the way through to the bottom of Carters Hill, which is just on the coast side of the Anawhata turn-off. The driving was done by my father, Wally Farley and me, and in May my father and mother went to Rotorua for a holiday.

Betty Atkin dressed to scare the photographer and then some, 1933!

My father and mother on holiday in Rotorua, May 1931.

Some of the hardest driving of my life was put in that winter. The chains had to be taken off at Carters Hill, put in a sugar bag and hidden in the bush for the return trip. I remember on one occasion my lights went out in the Nihotupu Valley and I had five of these men on, so had to drive up close behind Wally to get a bit of light from his tail light. We put the chains on at the bottom of Carters Hill without eating any carrots to see what we were doing and the only encouragement blending with the night atmosphere came from the bush in a shrill voice — morepork.

After getting the chains on I drove on through the mud from there to Karekare and down The Cutting with only a glimmer of light from his tail light. My eyes got used to the dark and with my knowledge of the road I knew just where to change gear and which set of ruts to take. When I got to the bottom of The Cutting the men all said they would go anywhere with me and never for a moment did they doubt my ability to get through, even without the glimmer of light from Wally Farley's tail light.

Even now I can see myself sitting in that 1925 Essex, crawling up Darkey's Hill in low gear with two wheels on the water table so as to keep the other two out of the deep ruts and mud in the middle. One of the trouble spots was much closer to home, just up from The Cutting Bridge. One Sunday

142   The Iron-Bound Coast

On the pohutukawa tree are (from left to right): Ron Muir, June Farley, Kathleen Farley, Neil Farley, Douglas Farley and, at top right, Eileen Badham, 1930.

afternoon when Wally Farley and I set off to go and get the men, he got bogged there with the 1926 Hudson. After a struggle we got him out and he went up round the next bend and then walked back to help me. I decided not to go in to the deep ruts but to put the two wheels on my side up on the edge of the road, and the other two in between the deep ruts. He did not know what my intention was and watched in amazement from the side as I flashed past him with the mud from the chains being flung about 10 feet in the air.

A love of flight

After my father and mother returned from Rotorua, father was back on the job again so it was all three of us each week of that notorious winter. While at Glen Eden one Sunday afternoon waiting for the men to arrive, an aero club plane flew over and my interest in the De Havilland Gipsy Moth began.

My father had noticed me looking at the plane as it flew over and asked if I would like to go out to Mangere some time. So, on the Sunday of Queen's Birthday weekend, we went out and stopped to pick up my brother, John, from Dilworth School, who was allowed out for the afternoon. After watching the flying and talking to the Grand Engineer Flying Officer R.J. Copley, I decided to join the Auckland Aero Club. We continued talking about it all the way home.

Early in August I received a letter from the Aero Club Secretary, Mr L.W. Swan, which I was to hand in to the instructor, Flight Lieutenant D.M. Allan. I would then be ready to start my flying training.

On a fine sunny morning I left home in the 1925 Essex and was going to stay at the clubhouse for two weeks. I handed the letter to Mr Allan and he said I could go up as many times a day as I liked but he recommended a half-hour in the morning and a half-hour in the afternoon. I replied I would leave it to him, so that was the way it was.

The clubhouse manager, Mr Treanor, was very kind and set out to help me all he could, knowing that I was the youngest member and about to start my flying training. He said he would put all my money in his safe and I could get what I required at any time. The first instruction was going to cost £3 10 shillings an hour and it was 2 guineas a week for members to stay at the clubhouse.

After settling in it was not long till lunchtime, so I did not get up till the afternoon. I think it was about 2 o'clock. After saying, 'We will go up now, Badham,' the instructor, Allan McGruer, called to one of the mechanics to start up the plane, ZK-AAU No. 1131. Allan McGruer, who was to become a great friend of mine, always referred to his students by their surname.

With the plane warmed up I put on my helmet, which turned out to be not the best as it was only a motorbike helmet with the DH phones put in. These were plugged in to a socket and you spoke into a tube with the reply coming back in your earphones. At that time it was hard to get a good helmet and I had to manage with it through my training. I had a job to hear what he was saying above the roar of the engine and wind. I still have this helmet and had about 20 hours solo before better ones, designed for flying, came on the market.

I got into the back cockpit, which is the pilot's seat. He stood beside me and the only thing he mentioned was the oil gauge; if the pressure dropped we would get down as soon as possible. He got into the front cockpit and started taxiing into the middle of the aerodrome, where he turned into the wind and took off over the clubhouse. Now remember, I had not been up since that day at Rotorua with Captain M.C. McGregor, 16 months ago. At 2000 feet he demonstrated the controls and I was having trouble hearing what he was saying; you can imagine how much better it would have been if he had explained everything on the ground first, not just the oil gauge.

I was that intent on trying to keep it straight and level that I had no time to look over the side to see where I was going. A quick glance and everything looked the same, a mass of paddocks and I had no idea where we were. Soon the lesson was over and he came in and landed close to the hangar.

The weather was perfect for the full two weeks and they all said, 'By gosh if ever we want good flying weather we will ring up and get you to come through.'

The old hangar was right across in the far corner of the aerodrome and you had to walk over from the clubhouse. It was one of Allan's little jokes if he was up with a pupil to wait till you were in the middle of the drome, with nowhere to go, to dive on you and force you to lie flat on your stomach as he roared overhead. We all got to know this and pupils who had come out for a lesson would have a good look round to see where he was before starting to cross the aerodrome.

I began to learn landing when I could fly straight and level, do turns with the engine on and off, as well and take off. One afternoon my father and mother arrived to see how I was getting on. As soon as Allan saw them he asked for ZK-AAU to be started up and called for me to get my helmet. He knew they had come to watch me and out we went. I had just taken off and was doing a 45° turn over Peacock's Island and looking down the wing at Peacock and another chap cutting scrub in a gully, when the voice in my earphones said. 'Let me take her.' Down we went in a screaming dive, forcing the Peacock and the other man to lie flat on their stomachs in the scrub. Peacock stood up and shook his fist at us. We shot skyward out of that gully and into a stall turn. My mother and father, who saw us go down and disappear from sight, thought we had crashed.

When we came in my father said to Allan, 'My word you gave us a fright.' He chuckled and I said I think the scrub-cutter got a bigger one. That night at dinner everyone heard about it and Peacock, who was sitting at the next table looked at me and said, 'So it was you that was with him in it. Just you wait.' Mrs Treanor had also seen us go down and she was out at the clothes-line and said it looked like we had gone slap into the Manukau. My father and mother returned home convinced I was in the hands of a very skilled pilot. About three days later my training was interrupted for a while and I returned home to help with the farm and driving.

My first solo flight

On the morning of 11 November, after doing the milking and doing breakfast, I set off alone for Mangere. I arrived in time for morning tea and they said, 'Welcome back Wally, and have you brought good weather with you again?' D.M. looked at me and said, 'I suppose you have forgotten all I taught you,' and I replied, 'I hope not.'

With tea over he said to me to get my helmet and McGruer went to start ZK-AAU. I took off and soon had the feel of it again as I came round for the landing. The half-hour was soon up and I taxied back to the hangar. As we got out he commented, 'That was quite good and better than I had expected.'

The next day I did two half-hour lessons and the landings were getting good. Next morning, 'the big day', Friday 13 November 1931. It was a nice morning but the wind was from the northeast, which meant coming in behind the clubhouse. We went out about 10:20 and did four landings, all good ones; suddenly I seemed to have it.

I put my hand on the throttle to open up and take off again and then heard Allan's voice in my headphones. 'No, taxi back to the hangar.' I got out and started to take my helmet off and he said, 'Don't take your helmet off, Badham. I want you to come up in this other machine.' That was ZK-AAK No. 915; my good friend McGruer was already refuelling it.

I now knew what was coming as other pilots had told me when Allan changed you over to another plane you were getting near it. Out we went and I did three landings to get the feel of this aircraft. They were all good and I was about to go off again when he said, 'How do you feel for a bit of solo?' I knew that all eyes would be on me but had confidence, remembering what he had said: 'You will have to be 100 percent.' I replied in a firm voice, 'I think I will be all right, Mr Allan.'

He stood by my cockpit and gave me a final word of advice, after which he stepped back and said, 'Right off you go.' He turned his back and walked away to the hanger. A quick check of the wind to make sure it had not changed and my left hand went to the throttle and opened it full. The tail came up, the ground rushed away and I was over the estuary with an

Flight Lieutenant D.M. Allan

Born in Waipukurau, D.M. Allan left New Zealand at an early age with his parents to settle in the Falkland Islands. At the out break of World War I he was domiciled on a cattle ranch in Tierra del Fuego, 'The land of fire', at the bottom of Patagonia. He used to have hanging in his office a big pair of spurs that he brought back from this South American cattle ranch.

He moved to England where he enlisted with the Royal Flying Corps, as it was known then. After gaining his wings he was posted as an instructor. While in this branch of the service he gave over 250 hours of dual instruction on Avros and Camels at Hounslow and Eastchurch. Some pilots would refrain from doing a right-hand turn with the Camel as they would easily go into a spin in that direction. I remember him telling me of an Australian pilot named Armstrong who used to flick-roll a Camel at the height of the hangar eaves. He spent most of the war as an instructor and had just completed a special fighting course at Massaka and was ready to go overseas when the Armistice was signed on 11 November 1918.

Returning to New Zealand, he took up sheep farming in Hawke's Bay. His wife came from Clive, between Napier and Hastings. When the aero clubs were being formed in February 1928 he came back to flying and was coming to Auckland to replace Major G.A.C. Couper, the first instructor. Major Couper used to put his pupils in the front cockpit and they never saw the back cockpit, which was the pilot's seat in the Gipsy Moth, till the day they went solo. The first three to be trained by him were Tom Philcox, E.B. and G.M. Firth, all of whom did dual from the front cockpit. When Allan arrived to take over he commented he would have none of that and that the pupil would sit in the pilot's seat right from the start.

So the change took place at Mangere, a new instructor with a new method. He used to draw large crowds to Mangere for his aerobatic displays, every Sunday afternoon at 4 p.m. I remember the day that Lord Malcolm Douglas Hamilton, the first pilot to fly over Mt Everest, was visiting Mangere, and Allan put on a display for him. When it was over and Lord Hamilton was asked what he thought of it, he replied, 'Well, he has done everything but fly down the clubhouse chimney and you wouldn't see anything better at the big Hendon airshow.'

Allan was New Zealand's leading stunt pilot in the 1930s and 1940s. I thought I had seen everything that it was possible to do until late one Sunday evening. Flying had finished for the day and the crew who had all watched the 4 o'clock aerobatic display had all gone up to the clubhouse and the planes were all being put in the hangar for the night. There were about 20 minutes of daylight left and suddenly a plane started up and I looked out of the window in amazement. Who could be going up now? It was ZK-AAU and D.M. was taking off. Taking off across the wind straight out from the hanger, he brushed the grass with the right wingtip as he left the ground in a climbing turn and coming round in a tight turn he got into the wind and came straight for the clubhouse. By this time everyone was at the windows and it looked as if he would clear the roof by about 25 feet. In sheer amazement we all stared as there he was right in front of the windows for about two minutes, not going over the roof. He had the aircraft perfectly balanced and just sitting in the wind, which was about a steady 20 mph, deftly manipulating the throttle so that it did not stall or go forward or backward. How about that. This is the only time and he is the only pilot I have ever seen perform this remarkable manoeuvre.

empty cockpit in front. I throttled back to 1800 rpm at 500 feet and looked down at the Chinamen in the gardens below. Then a look at the altimeter, gosh, 1000 feet and still climbing. No wonder, with me only about 8 stone and a 100 hp engine in front of me, a plane worth £800 with me only 16, the youngest ever. I throttled back to 1700 rpm and thought, 'What would Mum think if she knew that I was up here alone.'

A look back over the tail at the tiny speck that was D.M., also solo on his walk back to the hanger. I thought, 'Now, time for the normal procedure', and went into a left turn and looked down at the hangar. No one in sight as I expected and I could just imagine how the entire place had stopped as the word went round. The only things moving were me in ZK-AAK and D.M., now nearly back to the hangar.

I was now round behind the clubhouse and starting my approach going into the S-turns and trying to forget that all work had ceased in both the hangar and clubhouse. Out of the last turn, at about 100 feet and into wind as I watched the ground coming up, at the right moment I started to flatten off. The ground was close now and I knew the wheels were only about two feet off. The control column, which had been slowly coming back, now came back hard into my stomach and the wheels and tail-skid all touched down together in a perfect three-point landing. I was not the least bit thrilled as it seemed that the right moment for it had come.

I could still see no-one and knew that Allan would not let anyone outside, so I opened the throttle and took off again. Up I went with the same rapid climb; I was getting used to the empty cockpit in front now and came in for another good landing. Off I went again and looked down at the deserted aerodrome and thought to myself that as long as I was going round it would stay that way.

As I touched down in the third landing I thought I had better go in or the windows would break under the inside pressure. I taxied back to the hangar and D.M. came out and congratulated me. Then they were all out, including my good friend Leo White, the *Herald* photographer, who took the photos and had them in the *Herald* the next morning.

I now went up to the clubhouse as it was 11:45 a.m. so I just had time to put a ring through to Karekare before lunch. My mother answered the phone and I said, 'I have just been solo.' 'Oh, goodness, are you all right?' was her reply. I told her I was fine. I wondered about the responsibility D.M. had when he sent pilots solo but he said, 'When I send a chap solo there is no need to watch him.' Mum kept saying she couldn't believe it and I told her to watch for tomorrow's paper.

More events

Three more first solos were to come and it was my turn to join the crowd inside looking out the window. The first of the three was my good friend Leo White. He little knew then that he would have to make that walk four times that day. An all time record as never before had there been four solo flights in one day; a marvellous thing for the club as it was Aviation Week. After Leo had taxied back to the hangar and got out all smiles, I was next to D.M. to congratulate him.

I now went up to the clubhouse as a ring had come from there to say that Mr Treanor (clubhouse manager) who was out when I was up would like to see me. Just as I reached the door our leading lady pilot, the capable Miss Gwen Peacock, got in ahead of Mr Treanor with her congratulations. She had started some time ahead of me and had about 30 hours up. At the same time D.M. had started to walk to the hangar and I wondered who it was this time. After he had made his last landing and was coming in, Miss Peacock and I walked down to the hangar to see who it was. As the pilot got out we both could see that it was Mr R.G. Tappenden. None of us knew then that this remarkable day had more to come, with one more solo and the arrival of the first Air Mail from Invercargill to Auckland. The pilot was none other than my old friend of Rotorua days, Captain M.C. McGregor, in the Spartan ZK-ABZ.

He had left Invercargill early in the morning, landing and picking up mail at Dunedin, Oamaru, Timaru, Christchurch, Blenheim, Wellington, Palmerston North, Wanganui, Hawera, New Plymouth, Hamilton and Mangere. Before his arrival the fourth solo for the day was Mr R. Kemp of Hamilton.

With Mr Kemp safely down and everyone allowed to come out of the hanger, D.M. said to me, 'You had better go up again Badham.' So back I go into the cockpit of ZK-AAK and for the second time that day was alone in the sky for another half-hour. I had just landed and got back to the hangar when the Spartan ZK-ABZ was spotted coming low across the Manukau. I looked up as it circled the drome and could see that the door of the front cockpit had come open and the top of one of the mail bags was flapping in the slipstream. The front cockpit was full of mailbags and who ever put the last one in could not have closed the door properly. There was great revelling in the clubhouse that night and it was a tremendous boost for the club.

I stayed on at the clubhouse for another week as I had to do five hours solo before going for my pilot's A licence. After breakfast the next morning I saw McGregor off on his return to Palmerston North before going out for some more practice. The other three were all busy getting in the necessary five hours as well and we were all ready by the following Friday, 20 November 1931. D.M. had arranged with Squadron Leader L.M. Isitt, Officer Commanding Hobsonville Air Base, to come over and test us. All four of us were sitting on a seat outside the hangar looking over our air traffic rules as D.M. was going out with a pupil. He saw us and called out, 'What would you do if you saw a plane flying backwards?' Quick as lightning, Mr Tappenden replied, 'Put some more water with it.' We all laughed, as well as D.M.

About an hour later Major Isitt landed and he and D.M. sat in D.M.'s car and watched us all go through our paces. I can't remember the exact order in which we went out, except that Leo White went first and I was last so was able to taxi back to the hanger after. We had to do five figure-eights at 600 feet between two given points, then two landings, one from 1000 feet and the other from 2000 feet, without using the engine and finish within 50 yards of a circle in the middle of the aerodrome. Now to understand this you should know that a plane had no wheel brakes and you had to gauge just how far you would go after touching down. After my last landing from 2000 feet, when she came to rest the tail-skid and four feet of the fuselage were inside the circle. D.M. said, 'Very good' and Major Isitt commented it was 'A great show'. Back in the hanger we discussed it all and of course D.M. knew what we would do if we saw a plane flying backwards.

That night was the end of Aviation Week and a big dance was held in the clubhouse. The four of us were presented with our wings by Mrs G.R. Mason, wife of the president of the club. To me it was a far bigger ordeal than going solo, to have to go up and stand there in front of about 200 people and receive my wings from her, being only 16, and then make a speech. Somehow I got through it and was then congratulated by the aviation officers of the Shell and Vacuum Oil companies who were at the dance. My father and mother had come through for the big event and after it was over we left for Karekare, getting home about 1 a.m. I now had to get my feet back to earth as the busy season for us was coming on and I would have to help with the driving and farm work.

1932

Captain J.D. Hewett

In January of 1932, about the 20th, we still had over 30 staying in the house. Many of them were interested in my achievement and wondered if a plane could land on the beach so they could all have a flight before going home. The next day I went through to Mangere and discussed it with the Ground

Captain Hewett's Gipsy Moth at his aerodrome on top of Orakei Hill, 1930.

The first two passengers to go up were Mrs M.M. Farley (age 76), then Mr R. Shaw, a chemist from Remuera (age 84). They were the two oldest passengers for the day.

Engineer F/O R.J. Coley as D.M. was away. In D.M.'s absence I suggested we approach Captain J.D. Hewett, who lived at 65 Shore Road, Remuera, and had his aerodrome on top of Orakei Hill. That night I rang Captain Hewett and he said he would come over. I told him the tide was low about 11:30 a.m. He said he would bring a *Herald* photographer over.

I went down the next morning and made a fire, putting on a couple of old tyres to give black smoke for him to see the direction of the wind. He came down the coast and landed about 11 a.m. Just about everyone was on the beach to see the first landing of an aeroplane. I went over to greet them and found it was not Leo White with him but another *Herald* photographer I knew, Mr Audrey Breckon. As there were over 30 people wanting flights, Captain Hewett had to get going right away to get them all in and leave before the tide got back too far. They all got a flight; that day was the beginning of many days that he landed on the beach through that month of January 1932.

I was very busy putting the safety belts round each passenger, and then on the wingtip helping him to turn each time before taking off. After the last one had come in he said to me, 'You have been doing a lot of work, what about coming up before I go?' So we went off on the last flight of the day along to Whatipu and back over Pararaha; it was the first time I had seen these parts from the air. Just before leaving he said to me he could land beside The Watchman on the edge of the creek if it was clear of objects; this he did several times when the tide was in.

The crowd around the plane after landing.

Those up at the house would see the plane come low over the roof, then past the tennis court and below the level of Laurie Farley's cottage on The Watchman, before touching down on the edge of the lagoon. This he did quite often as guests for the house were now coming from Orakei in 10 minutes and landing beside The Watchman with the tide in. When we saw the plane come low over the roof of the house we went down with the Dodge truck to get the passengers and their luggage.

On one of these days my mother had come down in the Dodge with me to meet a guest and Captain Hewett asked her if she would like to go back with him for dinner and one of us could go through in the evening and bring her back. She jumped at the chance and really enjoyed the flight over, talking about it for days after.

A few days later I went through to Mangere for a couple of days to do a bit of flying myself. On one day I was just getting into the cockpit of ZK-AAL to go out when I saw ZK-AAR coming in. I knew it was Captain

Myself (age 17), Captain J.D. Hewett and my father on the beach the day Captain Hewett brought his plane to Karekare.

The first air mail was delivered to Karekare on 13 May 1932. Mr Laurie Farley had arranged to go to New Plymouth with Captain Hewett and they circled the valley and dropped a newspaper with a card of Captain Hewett's tucked inside. The paper landed in a paddock in front of the lawn.

Uncle Wally bringing firewood to the main house. Each month tons of wood would be used for heating and cooking. Uncle Wally left the family home to run the Whatipu Guest House to the south of Karekare.

Hewett and was very surprised to see his passenger was my grandmother; they had left Karekare beach 10 minutes earlier. She had decided to come down and stay at the clubhouse with me and watch me with my flying. I did two hours that day and had to watch my finances as it cost me 30 shillings for an hour and 2 guineas a week in the clubhouse. To do all this flying during the Depression and get my licence for carrying passengers, which required 40 hours of solo flying and then the test at Hobsonville, was financially no mean feat.

Back at Karekare and we still had about 20 guests in the house early in February. I had a ring one morning from Captain Brake, who had a World War I Avro 504K three-seater and wanted to know if we had any passengers. I said 'yes' and if he came over I would get them all down to the beach. He landed early in the afternoon and they were going up two at a time.

Not long after getting our first airmail, my Uncle Wally Farley and Aunt Florrie, with their family, decided to leave Karekare and take on running the old guest house at Whatipu. The day they left they took all their things down to the Point in the Dodge truck and had to carry them over the rocks and put them on a sledge on the other side. Our family did not see much of them for a while so it meant a lot more work for me on the Karekare property, as my brother Dudley was still at school till the end of the year.

As the cows came in I had to do most of the milking, getting them in and looking for any that had calves in the bush. I was kept very busy and only managed to get to Mangere for a flight once a fortnight. The winter gradually went by and on a nice fine sunny spring morning on 9 September 1932, I left on my own in the 1927 Essex for Mangere. I did not tell anyone what my intentions were, for it was to be my first flight from Mangere aerodrome to Karekare and back. Arriving at Mangere about 10.30 a.m. I asked for my favourite plane, ZK-AAL No. 866, which was painted with a red and cream check and looked quite attractive in the air with the silver wings. The day looked good as I climbed into the cockpit and took off into a south-west wind and climbed over the Manukau, then a left turn and headed straight for the Manukau Heads. The altimeter soon showed 3000 feet as I passed Onehunga on my right and Puketutu Island. Then came Blockhouse Bay, Ward Bay, Green Bay, French Bay, Titirangi Beach, Parau, Laingholm, Cornwallis and Huia.

The Karekare Valley as I saw it from the air on the morning of 9 September 1932.

Kare Kare Bay. West Coast. F.G.R. 5230.

Beautiful Union Bay and the North Rocks, known in the boarding house days as the Fishing Rocks. Today the rocks are called Farley Point. This image was taken by well-known photographer Henry Winkelmann.

I started to lose altitude for a low run over the roof of the guest-house and my cousins at Whatipu. They got a surprise and came running out waving tea towels as I circled round again before heading along the beach past Pararaha. I now spotted a horseman between Windy Point and Pararaha so went back up to 1000 feet and kept over the breakers so as not to frighten the horse. As I looked down I could see it was my Uncle Wally on a white horse. I learned later that he did not see me but said the horse looked up. I then looked down on the tunnel at Pararaha and thought of the many times I had gone through it on foot and horseback over the years and now, at 17, I was flying past it. Then came Mt Zion, 900 feet, and I was just 100 feet above it. When I was opposite and with Paratahi under my port wing, I did a right turn to go over the Black Rocks and then left to pass over the house and Flax Gully. Then I went between The Watchman and Fishing Rocks before coming round in another circuit.

By now the residents were all out waving tea towels. With a waggle of my wings I went back down the coast to Whatipu and passed over Wally

Farley again, still making his way along the beach. At Whatipu I roared over the house again and then circled round to climb up to 3000 feet for the trip back up the Manukau Harbour to Mangere.

As I approached the aerodrome I could see several more cars at the clubhouse, including Miss Gwen Peacock's Packard. I came round in a left-hand circuit and then closed the throttle and listened to the roar of the wind as I did my last S-turn and watched the ground coming up. Then at the right moment the wheels and tail-skid all touched the ground together in a perfect three-point landing.

At the hangar I made a turn into the wind beside the other planes as I was the only one who had been out and switched off. I was aware that many eyes were watching the landing and as I got out Gwen Peacock came over to greet me. She asked where I had been so I told her and she said they were getting worried because I had been away an hour. We talked on as we went up to the clubhouse for lunch and she said she would go up after lunch. I said I would have to go back then as I have to be home for the milking, so about an hour after leaving I was home again, this time with my feet on the ground. Even now, after all these years, I can still see Wally Farley on that white horse and the tea towels waving away at Whatipu and Karekare. The next day my cousins from Whatipu, Kathleen and Woee, came round and said I had given them all a surprise and they could not understand how their father had not seen or heard me, even though he was a bit hard of hearing.

As it got into November we were notified that the house would have to be rewired to meet insurance requirements so the work would have to be started right away to be finished before Christmas. A few days later two electricians arrived, a Mr Doug King and his assistant Mr E.J. Jimmy Stewart. They worked hard and had it all done in time. Jim Stewart stayed on as it was the Depression and he could not get any more work. At the same time it was decided to build a new garage for the two service cars in front of the powerhouse and a carpenter named Mr Allan Harper came to do the job. He and Jim Stewart became good friends with me and brother Dudley. When the garage was finished Allan wanted to stay on as well as he could not get any more building work. So they both helped through the season and into the winter of 1933, then the summer of 1933 and also the summer and winter of 1934. After the garage was finished a Shell petrol pump was installed by the Shell Company so we now had our own supply on the spot.

My father had the two cars, the 1927 Essex and the 1927 Buick, both painted black and red. Just after my eighteenth birthday I went to Glen Eden to meet Betty Atkin and her girlfriend Kathleen Tui, who were coming to work the season as waitresses. As they stepped off the train and walked over to greet me, both dressed the same in white blouse and blue skirt, I thought they looked dashing. They talked a lot on the drive back and both had heard of my flight over Karekare in the red Moth ZK-AAL. Although she didn't know it then, Betty was to be my second passenger after I obtained my passenger's licence in 1933.

We got along well that Christmas, the first without Wally Farley and his family. Jim and Allan learned how to keep the waitresses from waiting. On New Year's Eve, Jim, Betty, myself and another girl climbed right up on to the top of The Watchman to see the New Year in. Allan and Kath Tui with some others were somewhere at sea level. As we sat there waiting for midnight I thought of the terrible massacre that had occurred on that very spot in the 1820s; all we had to suffer were the Depression years.

1933

The new year was only about a week old when Betty's sister Olive, who had been staying on a farm at Coromandel, came home. They had given her a young cattle dog and she realised that she could not keep it in town and asked Betty if I would like to have it for the farm. So the next day I had to do a trip to town in the Buick and went out to Maungakiekie Avenue, Mt Eden to get him. I called him Wolf and he was very fond of me and would not work for anyone else.

About a week later I had to go into the Waitemata County Office in Princess Street to get four men who were coming out to work on the road. They were Relief workers and this time I had the 1927 Essex for the trip. When I got back with them, Allan, Jim and my brother Dudley, who were all getting firewood out of the steep bush, came down to help them put up the tents in the paddock below The Cutting Bridge. The four tents had corrugated iron chimneys so they could have an open fire. There were getting to be a lot of Relief workers round the Waitakere Ranges; they were known as 'The Number 5 Scheme'.

Tents belonging to the relief workers that would travel to the West Coast to work in the Waitakere Ranges.

A governess for my sister Eileen

The Karekare school closed down at the end of 1932 and my mother and father had to get a governess for Eileen. She was Miss Vincent, who remained with us all through 1933. I remember one startling event that happened when my father and I were going to Glen Eden in two separate cars. I had the 1927 Essex with Miss Vincent as passenger, and my father was driving the Essex 4 truck.

We had come down a hill in Oratia, with my father in front and me following. At the bottom was a one-way concrete bridge with the road climbing up on the other side. I should state here that all cars in those days

Karekare School, 1927. From left: Kathleen Farley, Wally Badham, Keith Rule, Wallace Farley Jnr (nickname 'Woee'), Ron Rule, Dudley Badham, June Farley, Neil Farley, John Badham and Douglas Farley.

Miss Jessie Alexander.

had only two wheel-brakes and were not like modern speedsters with one on each wheel.

I always kept a safe distance behind the car in front and a sharp eye on the road ahead. Just as my father got near the bridge I spotted a car coming fast down the hill. The driver must have realised that he could not get over in time and was going too fast to stop. I had changed down into second to go down the hill and was well under control as I watched him charge off the road through long grass into a clump of wattles, stopping just short of the creek. It was the only thing he could have done or he would have collided on the bridge with my father. I got out to see if he was hurt and if the car could be driven back on to the road. The driver was not hurt and was able to get back on to the road. We carried on to Glen Eden and loaded up for the return trip.

Miss Vincent had to leave at the end of that year. Miss Ross came for 1934 and she and Betty Atkin were both with us that winter when the big flood in June floated the far bungalow off its blocks. Miss Ross left at the end of the year and the next to come was a young girl called Joan Davies from Kakahi King Country, in February 1935. Joan's people wanted her home at the end of 1935, so in 1936 there was another governess. Early in February of 1936, Miss Jessie Alexander of Waverley arrived for the remaining two years' of Eileen's schooling. Miss Alexander was later to become my sister-in-law and settle in the big city of Auckland.

It was quite a busy summer in spite of the Depression, for it seemed that people still have to have a holiday even if the butcher, baker, grocer and candlestick maker are cashing in their chips. I had to do a lot of the driving and was often doing three trips a day in and out of Auckland, for my father had just started collecting people from their homes. Imagine finding your way to a street in Herne Bay, then over to Parnell and back through Remuera and Mt Albert. On all these trips I was never late at any of these places. My mother always said I had missed my calling and should have been an engine driver.

Just before Easter I heard from my cousins at Whatipu that Mr Muir the chemist, who used to come and stay in the house quite a lot, had bought the Pararaha farm from Mr Jack Lawrence of Huia, for his son Ron. All that winter he was using packhorses to bring in supplies along the top of the cliffs on the Morningside Timber Company road.

Ron used to come out and stay with his people in the house quite a bit and I knew him well. His father had 75 acres cleared at the back of the gorge and fronting on to the Morningside Timber Company Road. They then burnt it and sowed grass seed and had it fenced with beautiful fencing, far too good for that type of country. I did not see much of Ron in the first three years he was at Pararaha till he moved down into the gorge in January 1936 and into a slab hut built by Fred Gibb in 1930.

With Easter over we were going into the winter and Betty Atkin and Allan Harper were still with us. Jim Stewart had gone home for a few weeks as he had a bit of work to do. So one night in July, with a bit of light rain falling and about 7:30 p.m., we were all in the kitchen when suddenly the light went out. I dashed out, followed by Allan, thinking that an eel had come down the pipe, but outside I could see a big red glow and quickly called out, 'The powerhouse is on fire!'

We all dashed down and Allan and I knocked a bung out of a six-inch pipe and put a sheet of corrugated iron over the huge jet of water, setting it to direct the water into the heart of the fire. We got it out but all that was saved was the pelten wheel and some of the short timber and pulleys. It was no accident for a firebug was round and it had been decidedly set on fire with the night carefully chosen.

We now had no electric light or circular saw to cut the firewood and a start had to be made right away clearing up the mess and rebuilding. Fortunately Allan was a carpenter and we all worked from daylight till dusk. I think it was about a couple of weeks later that we had a light going again, for my father had managed to get a generator from Lunar Park, which had just closed down. Jim Stewart came back and did all the electrical work; this generator was 230 volts so we were the same as Auckland now. The old one was 110 volts and the second one to be imported into New Zealand.

About the middle of September we had another fire, this time in the cottage by the powerhouse that used to be the home of Wally Farley and his family. Allan, Jim, Dudley and I used to sleep in it and Allan called it the 'Vicarage'. At this time Allan and Jim were not with us, having gone back home to try and get work. On this night I think my brother Dudley must have been reading with a candle and fallen off to sleep. I woke in the early hours of the morning feeling something was wrong and found the wall on fire. I got out of bed and pulled him out and made the mistake of telling him to get what he could out while I ran over to the house to give the alarm.

When I got back with my father and all the others, who had been woken up by my mother, were running down the road in their nightgear behind us. The cottage was well ablaze. To my amazement Dudley had got nothing out and was just standing there as if he had seen a witch take off on a broomstick. This was my mistake; I should have sent him and I could have got quite a lot out. We lost quite a bit I am afraid, including some early photos that I would have liked for this book.

With everyone now on the spot, a bucket brigade was formed from the creek to the fire. I was at the creek filling the buckets and handing them to Betty Atkin. The water slopping on the ground made it very slippery and after about 10 minutes she swung round to hand me another bucket and her feet shot from under her. In she went, pyjamas and all. As she shot past me I grabbed her arm and I nearly went in as well, but I dug my heels in and pulled her out. Although she was sopping wet she refused to go and change and kept on handing the buckets along the line.

The heat was now terrific and I think her pyjamas were about half dry when the bargeboard on the garage caught alight from the heat. I yelled, 'Quick get the cars out,' as I tackled the new threat with a garden hose. Fortunately there was no wind. With the two cars out nothing could be done except play the hose on the garage, the side of which was corrugated iron. Laurie Farley and myself stayed on guard after everyone else had gone back to bed.

Another harrowing event was not a fire, but the crashing down of the big macrocarpa tree in front of the big bungalow during an 'equinox gale' at the end of September. It was a big job cutting and sawing it up into firewood and fenceposts and it took weeks. You can imagine what the lawn looked like with sawdust, chips and bootmarks in the soft grass.

The big bungalow and macrocarpa tree, Christmas 1930.

On the last day of September, a Thursday, we were just finishing dinner when in walked Bill McMaster, the racehorse man, whose horse Clive my mother had trained on the beach in 1907. He had walked from Glen Eden and spent the night at Andy Lloyd's place at Waiatarua. Andy was one of the old coach drivers.

I had just got my licence and logbook back from Wellington that day and I had planned to take my mother and Betty Atkin to Mangere the next day to be my first passengers. McMaster said, 'You go as you had planned and I will see you when you get back.' It was a lovely day and they both enjoyed the flight in the red Moth ZK-AAL, with my mother first and then Betty. Back at Karekare the old days were lived again each night as McMaster and my mother recalled different events.

It had been eventful year, enough to try the patience of Job, to say nothing of the jobs. Now it was Christmas again and we had an influx of tourists but we would have preferred the quiet to the rush. McMaster stayed on and was to help through that summer.

In those days we often got what the old settlers called the Kowhai Flood in October. Later on in the 1940s these just seemed to fade away.

At the foot of what we called Fluming Hill was a triangular-shaped piece of land with the road on one side and a 12-foot right of way and then the creek on the other. This would be about the tightest bit of land in New Zealand at the time and at the base of the hill Allan put up a small building for us that had a copper for boiling water for the day trippers and was also a shop. This was nicknamed the Soup Kitchen.

One Saturday in early 1933 I took Mr and Mrs Wilcocks for a flight; they were two of our regular passengers. Mrs Wilcocks brought her brother, Athol and his girlfriend, Betty. It was quite a busy day, with a lot of pilots wanting to fly and some of the planes away on cross-country flights, so we were only allowed a quarter of an hour each, which meant I could only take one of them up.

It was decided that Athol's girlfriend should be the one. I could have flown off with her but the others knew I couldn't go far with a quarter of an

The soup kitchen, 22 January 1934.

The end of the macrocarpa

My first memory of the big macrocarpa that stood in front of the house long before we were there, was seeing it on the morning I took a ride in Sandfly with Mr Jack Sergeant in 1918. At this time my godmother, Mrs R. Eyre, and Mr R. Eyre were looking after the place while my grandparents were in America. They were there when the Armistice was signed on 11 November 1918. As with the Lone Kauri, I can not give the actual day that it was felled, but I am sure it was just after Easter 1938. As the big bridge just next to it had to be replaced, it was decided to have it cut down and taken to Odlin Mill at Glen Eden to be cut into suitable timber for the job.

Once cut Mr Laurie Wilson drove the truck and trailer carrying it to the big log mill at Glen Eden. As the old bridge would not take the tree's weight, the log had to be rolled in to the creek and then pulled up the bank on to the road by the big truck. This took a while.

With the log on the road, the next part was to jack it up on to the trailer with timber jacks. You can imagine the climb up The Cutting with that load. The big truck had eight forward gears and would be in bottom gear getting up Slippery Rock, with its one in four grade.

Not many people today would realise that the big macrocarpa supplied all the timber for the bridge that was still there on 1 May 1973.

This photo of me and Betty Atkin's sister, Olive, was taken not long after I took Betty Wilcocks and the others out to Mangere, 1935.

hour time limit. I was 20 at the time and she was passenger number 50. She said she was thrilled to bits with the flight. I gave her a very smooth landing. They talked a lot on the way back to Buckland Road and commented that, 'Your mother must be proud of you with four years flying behind you now.' I returned home on Sunday evening to Karekare knowing I had made a friend. Unfortunately Betty Wilcocks died of tuberculosis two years later, in 1937. I lost a good friend.

1934

Before we got to Easter the big camp of relief workers that had been situated between the top of the Karekare Cutting and Lone Kauri was now brought down to Karekare.

This camp, with cookhouse and huts, was directly opposite my second right paddock, on the edge of the road and just below the Black Rock and 40 acres. These men were going to widen what was known as the 6-foot track from below the big Cave Rock, up past Mothers-in-Law's Leap and the first and second Taraire gullies to Lone Kauri. I got to know them all. I was only 19 then. Through that winter we used to invite half a dozen at a time for the evening to play billiards on our small table.

With Easter over Betty Atkin stayed on for another winter and Jim and

The Six Foot Track being formed just past Mother-in-Law's Leap.

The view from Cave Rock looking out and across to the waterfall and flume. To the left, the little cluster of houses that were Wally's life. The boarding house and accommodation wings are around the edges of the lawn and the old hall sits on its original site.

Allan were coming and going as they could get a bit of work to do. Another job was coming up for us as the fluming from the top of the waterfall to the tank, 180 feet above the powerhouse, would have to be replaced. The fluming came for about 300 yards through the bush on trestles; the new timber 12x1 would have to be nailed together in the shape of a V and got up there. This was quite a job.

Having spent most of my life in the bush and on the sides of hills and often on precipices, I did not think of it other than an ordinary job. The two 12x1s were nailed together near the powerhouse after being treated with petroleum. Some were 14 feet long. I nailed most of these and carried them up the steep part to the edge of the bush on Flaming Hill. Imagine going up that steep bit with a 14 foot length on your shoulder and not being able to stop until you got to the top. They then had to be dragged from there up through the bush to the tank by myself, my father and my brother Dudley.

After we got the first two in place with a crosspiece at each end and one in the middle, the following one could be turned on its side and dragged over to the next place. In this way we worked our way through the bush to the head of the falls, using a spirit level to keep the grade right. The job had to be done a bit at a time as all the other work, such as getting the cows and milking, getting firewood and trips to Glen Eden, had to be done as usual.

The start of the track before it was formed, looking back to The Watchman.

In the image on the left you can clearly see the flume leading into the bush, it is not so evident in the photo on the right, 1904.

It took about a month to finish it and some days we could only spend a few hours in the afternoon carrying more lengths up from the bottom.

The next big job started on my mother's 45th birthday on 19 June 1934. We had been getting heavy rain all day and the creek was in full flood. About 2 p.m. the bungalow next to the paddock floated off its blocks and swung round towards the big bungalow. I happened to be watching at the time and saw the end nearest the creek swing round. Fortunately the rain stopped shortly after, allowing the creek to drop so we could assess the damage.

We decided it was no good putting it back where it was and as it consisted of six bedrooms it was too big to move in one piece. My father got hold of Allan Harper and he came out and said he would cut it in half. By using timberjacks, we could then jack it across the lawn and put it in two different places. We laid two 6x4s on the lawn, one at each end, and then put one in the middle. After putting grease on them and with the timberjacks on each corner of the building, we worked our way right across the lawn. The one half of three rooms went between the drawing room and the big bungalow and the other half just below it. All this took several weeks; June was not the best month to be doing it, with frequent wet days and often a cold wind blowing.

Allan was a good worker and we kept plodding along with it. The only spell I got was when it was time to go and get the cows. At last this part was in place and we had to raise it up to the correct height with bottlejacks, which we fortunately had among our hardware. When this was finished we had to start on the other half and repeat the performance. We did not have so far to go with this part but had to join it on to another room.

Allan stayed on for a few days of rest before going back to town. I took him up to the head of the waterfall to see the new flume that we had put in. He thought it was a mammoth job and asked me, 'Is there nothing you can't do? You drive from Waiatarua to Karekare through all the mud with no lights and then down The Cutting, fly a plane and take up passengers, including me, while you are still only a boy, and you get wild cattle out of the bush and get then to the saleyard at Henderson.' Those busy days are something to look back on now.

With Allan gone it was the usual routine of getting and cutting up firewood with the farm work. Through these years just about everyone on the coast except us had been trapping possum. This consisted of scrambling through the bush and setting traps, then going back the next morning to collect not the hardware but the fluffyware. They then had to be skinned and dried before they got the elusive pound for every single one of them.

An event of great interest to me and all the locals was to start on

Dudley and Eileen sitting on the veranda after the first part of the bungalow was put back in place.

Me at the top of Big Cone Rock looking across at the new flume and waterfall, 1934.

20 October — the Melbourne Centennial Air Race. A large number of planes took part and the race was run in two parts, the speed section and the handicap section. As I was the resident pilot everyone wanted to ask me what was it like in the air and could I see myself in the great race. To be honest I would have loved to have been part of it.

All the planes left Mildenhall Aerodrome, England on the morning of the 20th. The first to reach Singapore in a DH Comet was Squadron Leader C.W.A. Scott and Captain T. Campbell Black. They averaged 220 mph and then went on to Melbourne and won the race.

As we come to Labour Weekend my father traded the 1927 Buick in with Dominion Motors for a 1931 Essex. We now had the 1927 Essex and a 1931 Essex, which were the two service cars for a while.

The relief men were making good progress on the Six Foot Track. This would link the beach and the two guest houses and the Odlin Farm road. I used to like to go for a walk up there in the evenings and see how they were getting on. On the way back I sometimes went up onto the top of the Big Cave before returning. Mr C.A. Odlin used to say that his road from Lone Kauri would one day come right. He did not know then that it would not be until after we sold the farm in June 1950.

I used to wonder what the first great miller, Charles Murdoch, would think if he could see the dirt track being formed into a road after all the years he put in to cut the track, right up till 1886, in order to get the kauri out of that big gully. The way he did it was to dam the creek, then jack and roll the big logs into it and, with sufficient logs and a big enough head of water, trip the dam and the whole lot would come crashing down the cascades and land on the flat by his mill.

By November of 1934 I had taken up many passengers; most of them had never been up in a plane before. The oldest was a man of 78 and I felt proud to think that he wanted to go up with such a young pilot.

I felt great excitement when I found out that two chaps were flying the Tasman Sea in a Moth just like the one owned by the Auckland Aero Club. The chaps were Mr R.G. Whitehead, who had over 450 hours up with the RAAF, and Mr E.R. Nicholl. They took off from Sydney on the morning of 22 November and took 14 hours 40 minutes before landing on the beach at Doubtless Bay in the Far North, just before dark. They were aiming for Wellington but strong southerly winds had swept them north and they very nearly missed New Zealand altogether. Land was first sighted in the region of Ahipara Bay and they soon realised that they were in the Far North as they cruised over the beaches looking for the best place to get down before the light went.

No-one saw them land as Doubtless Bay was pretty isolated then. With darkness setting in anxiety for them spread through the country. The pilots could see a light from a farmhouse but could not get to it so decided to stay with the plane on the beach for the night. At daylight they took off and flew down the west coast to the Manukau Heads and then up the harbour to Mangere.

The 1931 Essex about to leave with the mail, 9 a.m., 1934.

The proud owner of a 1931 Essex, Dudley Badham Snr was more than happy to look the elegant gent on the Auckland waterfront.

I was up the Flax Gully looking for one of the cows and heard the plane and looked up. To my astonishment I saw that it was a Moth with the Australian registration letters, VH-UON, which I at once recognised. I was the first one to recognise them, many others would have seen them all the way down the coast but would not have known what VH-UON meant. I rushed back to get to the phone and ring Mangere, but by the time I got through my friend, the mechanic Allan McGruer, who answered the phone, said the plane was just landing.

The Six Foot Track below an arch of tarire trees.

The punga bridge crossing Taraire Gully.

1935

We got through the Christmas and New Year rush and it was about the middle of January when my father had to be rushed to hospital. He was down at the garage by the powerhouse doing something to one the cars when it slipped off the jack. He tried to get it up and must have strained himself for shortly after he was in great pain and my mother rang the doctor, who sent an ambulance out for him. They took him to Rawhiti Hospital in Mt Eden Road and got there just in time.

An operation was done by a Dr Pezaro and Dr Clive Low. Father was in hospital till about the middle of February. I now had to take my father's place and do all the carving at meal times as well as the driving of the service car, with the help of my brother Dudley, milk twice a day and get all the firewood down from the bush and cut it up. These tasks kept us very busy. Then there were the frequent trips up the fluming to keep the water coming to the powerhouse. After dinner at night either myself or Dudley had to take Mum into Mt Eden to see Father so that was another trip in and out.

The late summer went steadily on. With between 25 and 30 people in the house we were very busy. I can remember how I used to keep the two waitresses on the mark by leaving the carving to the last moment before going over and telling them, 'Three minutes to go, ladies.' So the gong went right on the dot of 6 p.m., just as my grandmother had insisted all through the years. One evening

Winchelsea Guest House, 1935.

when I had taken my mother in to hospital after dinner to see Father and as we were about to leave to come home, I overheard her telling him how I kept a sharp eye on the girls and that Grandma had long given up worrying that the gong would not go on time.

About the middle of February Father came home as a convalescent and did not get back to the driving till just before Easter. With him back on the road it took some of the pressure off me as driving the service car, looking after the farm and powerhouse as well as getting and cutting the ti-tree at the rate of a ton a day was no mean feat.

A sea rescue

It was 3 February 1935, an eventful day. The dramatic incident that follows is almost buried with the passing of time and the drifting of the black Karekare iron sand in the many years that have elapsed since the event. With my father sadly back in Rawhiti Hospital in Mt Albert Road, I had just returned from Auckland with a carload of guests for the house in the early afternoon. Before I had time to get out of the car several people rushed up to me and said a girl was drowning and was swept out beyond the breakers. They had tried to reach her with the Piha Surf Club line but she was out too far, and what could we do?

I was an aero club pilot with quite a lot of flying experience; I knew there were two Fairy III seaplanes at Hobsonville, and I knew Squadron Leader L.M. Isitt, the CO, and Flight Lieutenant S.G. Wallingford quite well. I made a quick decision and told Uncle Laurie Farley to ring Hobsonville and explain the situation and ask Squadron Leader Isitt if one of the seaplanes could come over. I then made a quick change into my home clothes and dashed up on to The Watchman to look and see if the girl was managing to keep afloat.

Shortly after the seaplane arrived and circled before touching down on the sea, which was fairly calm but undulating with a steady swell. I watched as Flight Lieutenant Wallingford taxied close to the breaker-line and LACA Palmer scrambled down on to the port float to throw a rope to the girl. He pulled her up to the float and held her there while Wallingford taxied out about 200 yards to get away from the breakers.

The next step was risky as Wallingford had to leave his cockpit and join Palmer on the float to help lift the limp girl from the sea. They struggled to get her through the biplane wires as they were being lashed with the slipstream from the big propeller; the plane was working its way round in circles all the time. After what seemed ages they got the girl up and I held my breath as the pilots headed into the wind for the take off. The run took about two miles with the extra weight and ground swell. Suddenly the spray stopped and they were away.

Back at Hobsonville they kept the girl warm till the ambulance arrived. Hazel Bentham was very lucky and so ended the first seaplane rescue of a swimmer from the West Coast surf.

Hazel Bentham, image taken around 1924.

These photos were taken from the same spot in 1896 and 1936 respectively. The first shows fishing in the creek in 1896. The second shows the cottage built in 1936 for A.G. Brown in front of the bent tree and above Laurie Farley's place.

Dancing on the lawn, New Year's Eve, 1935.

Autumn at Karekare: Eileen Badham in 1935.

I now had just the farm work to do on my own but went to Mangere once a fortnight to keep my hand in on the flying. I could only afford a half-hour a time as these were the Depression years, but it made a nice change from the usual routine.

Late in November of 1935, Mr A.G. Brown, General Manager of the Auckland Farmers Freezing Co., returned from an overseas trip and decided to build a place on his section on The Watchman in time for the Christmas holidays. It was a rush job and all the men, two carpenters, two plumbers, two painters and two labourers, stayed in the house with us while the job was being done. The two labourers had the hardest job as they had to carry everything up the hill for the other men. Just imagine going up and down the hill with all the heavy timber and other goods all day, for nine hours a day.

The job was done and all finished in just three weeks and Mr Brown and his wife, who was Miss Daisy Carter before her marriage, moved in with their family for the Christmas holidays. Her family used to live in a small house on the road just past McElwains Flat on the way to the coast. Hence the name Carter's Hill.

With the job finished the men all took part in the New Year's Eve gathering and dancing on the lawn before going back to town. It all seems a long time ago now though very fresh in my memory.

For Christmas 1935 we had the loan of a valve amplifier, which we set up at the bottom of the lawn to provide music for evening dancing. My father, Jim Stewart and myself also put a fountain in the centre of the lawn, which I must say looked very attractive as dusk fell. It had coloured lights set below the water.

New Year's Eve 1935 was a big event at Karekare, with dancing on the lawn in front of the fountain while the music from the amplifier could be heard up on Piha Road at the Ussher house. I could not dance then so did not take part, but watched it all from the front veranda, with frequent trips down to the powerhouse to see that the plant was running smoothly.

1936

It was the middle of January and as usual we were still very busy. One of the girls who came to work for the season was called Betty Cook. Some of the guests had been taking lunch and going round the beach to Whatipu for the day. Betty Cook had been listening to them talking about it and she thought she would go walkabout too, except alone.

I had been up in the bush getting ti-tree out and when I came in for morning tea and noticed that Betty was missing. I asked where she was and was told that she had gone to Whatipu for the day. I nearly choked over a biscuit and commented, 'Good heavens, I suppose that means all hands and the cook will be out looking for her tonight.' How right I was.

Dinnertime came and went and the daylight was wending its way. I decided we had better search for Betty. Three others said they would go with me, Olive Atkin, Miss M. Hawthorne of Wellington, and a former coach driver, Mr Gill Woods. Halfway across the bay to Karekare Point the daylight was starting to fade and I said to the others I could travel faster so I would go on ahead.

In the gathering gloom I could not pick up any tracks so decided to make straight for Whatipu. When I reached the house I met three of my cousins who had just come up from the wharf, Woee, June and Neil. I asked them if they had seen a girl and gave a description of Betty. She had been seen on the wharf having lunch but no one had seen her after that. My Uncle Wally Farley said we had better go and have a look round the rocks to the big cave at Windy Point. We set out with a lantern but all to no avail. I said to Woee and Neil that they better go back and I would search the beach on the way home.

Between Windy Point and Pararaha I met Gill Woods and the girls and told them the story. As we wondered what to do next, I could just see the silhouette of a man on a horse coming along the beach. I was not long in finding out who it was. As he drew level with us I recognised Ron Muir

Looking south from the Fishing Rocks, 1936.

from Pararaha. I greeted him and asked if he had seen anything of the girl as we were out looking for her. He said yes he had, that he had just taken her home and then he started to tell an amazing story. He had come in from work to get his evening meal and noticed just as it was getting dark that his dogs were acting strangely, running round and looking up at the steep cliffs that hem the Gorge in.

Puzzled by his dogs' actions, Ron went outside and looked up the sides of the cliffs and then he heard what sounded like a human voice, far above him. A second call and he spotted what looked in the fading light like a girl at the top of a waterfall over to the side and above his shack. If you look at the photo of the Pararaha Gorge in 1931, you can see the spot to the right of the dark patch in the top right corner, while the white patch to the right of the creek is Ron's shack. Ron called out to the girl to stay where she was till he could get up to her. He reckoned he 'had a father, no, a mother of a job' getting her down to his shack. She was a bit delirious and he had somewhat of a job trying to find out how she got up there.

He then told me she kept on repeating, 'Why did they make a road that doesn't start and doesn't finish?' This of course was the old Morningside Timber Co. Road that ran from the top of the cliffs at Whatipu and ended in the bush at the back of the Pararaha Gorge.

We all made straight for the house. I found my mother with Betty in the sitting room, trying to calm her while she kept repeating, 'Why do they make a road that doesn't start and doesn't finish?' Betty was sent back to her mother the next day as the other girls said they would manage without her.

On Saturday 13 June 1936, Mrs Phillipson of the Blow Hole, just south of Piha, started dancing lessons for us all. Living with them was Yvonne La Trobe, and on top of the hill there were the three Usshers: Betty, Phil and Owen. We used to go from there on to the Blow Hole each Saturday night, and later occasionally to an old cottage that we fixed up near Ussher's place. We sometimes had a bigger dance at either Karekare or Piha. This used to help to pass the winter away through 1936 and 1937, with supper provided we had many enjoyable evenings.

The summer of 1936 and early 1937 was as busy as usual and Jessie stayed and helped us with the rush, including the rescuing of any venturesome bathers who with no savvy thought that there is nothing between us and Australia.

The Lone Kauri

I think it was around August or September of 1936 that this tree was felled, as the photo tells me the 1931 Essex was doing the mail trip that morning. We did not have the 1929 Hudson at the time, but we did have it for the summer season.

Also in the photo is Mr Jack Odlin with his axe, standing in the road just in front of the Essex and behind him, hidden by the car door, we can just see a woman's foot, which I think is my mother's. I am sure she was in the car that morning as she wanted to see the last of the great tree that she had known since 1900.

This last paragraph I reserve for the memory of Mr Moffat Byles and the half-caste Maori, Mr Tommy Galter, who gave a climbing exhibition on the tree for members of the Waitemata County Council and their wives, in 1912.

My mother also watched that exhibition and told me how after they got up into the branches they took their climbing boots off. Then, with a short axe in their hands, they jumped from branch to branch, some 80 feet above the gully.

The Lone Kauri's final stand.

1937

Late in February 1937 I burnt a big part of Karekare Point on my own and kept it all under control. The total area of the Point was 180 acres. I timed it to perfection and was just getting ready to leave to come home when light rain started falling. In less than a week the area began to look green as the new grass began to come away; it was being eyed by the cattle that I had moved to the first part of the bush at the back in the meantime.

The Karekare gang. Badham family members and surf club regulars in the late 1930s.

In the autumn I took some of the guests in the 1929 seven-seater Hudson down to the Whatipu Dam for the day. The total area of the dam is 36 acres and it's a grand sight to anyone from the city. This was possible as I knew the ranger living there at the time, a Mr Davidson. As we all stood on top of the spillway and watched the water cascading down, the guests were spellbound. All too soon it was time to leave for home.

In late July a slip above the powerhouse brought most of the pipes in the 180-foot drop down to the bottom. The first three out from the powerhouse and the first two at the top were okay, but those in the middle had all been brought down in a tangled heap and were damaged. They were jarrrah, 16-feet long and came from Western Australia. With a Labour Government in office at the time that had imposed rigid import controls, we could not replace them.

The 180-foot drop was now a sea of mud and tangled bush. The only answer was concrete pipes, which we learned were four-feet long, seven in diameter and weighed 200-weight each. This was a real curse as the 16-foot jarrah pipes were only a fraction of that weight and 6 in diameter. This meant reducing joints from seven to six inches. To say nothing of getting the heavy 200-weight pipes up there.

Having ordered the pipes from the Hume Pipe Co., two men arrived with a truckload and the job was about to commence. Those two men, used to laying 170 a day in flat ground, nearly fainted on the spot and were only revived by a swarm of bees passing over looking for greener pastures. They were thunderstruck as they watched me go up the hill and cut a fork from a big ti-tree and bring it down to make the front of a sledge for the pipes to rest on.

No doubt they were thinking, 'if only we had sky-hooks.' My father read their thoughts and said he had seen the Indian rope trick in Calcutta where a man threw a rope up in the air then climbed up it and disappeared. I think they thought though that if they were to climb up the slip they would disappear 'in the mud' without the rope.

My father and I now got three 12x1s and cut them just over four-feet long. Two were placed on edge and the third lying flat was nailed to the sledge and the edges of the other two. This made a good place for the pipe to rest as it was dragged up the slippery face. It now looked like a long box and was made fast to the fork with four-inch nails and a piece of No. 6-gauge fencing wire and staples.

The next job was to place three snatch blocks in suitable positions for the rope to pass through. The first one went around the base of the big pohutukawa tree by the powerhouse, then the second one halfway up the hill and the third round a big ti-tree at the top.

We were now ready to start. One of the men tied one end of the rope to the truck. I then took the other end, which was 700 feet long, and passed it through the first snatch block and worked my way up through the mud to the second one. Having put it in to that one I carried on up the steep face to the one at the top, hanging on by the skin of my teeth, which I put it through. Then, turning round, looked down the 180-foot drop with the others far below, watching me. With one hand on the rope I worked my way down to the sledge.

The two men had been watching spellbound and were amazed that I was back in one piece. Having accepted that this was the case they now helped to put the first pipe in the box.

The driver now got in the truck and drove straight out towards the sea. As the sledge started to move up the side of the jarrah pipes, my father, my brother Dudley and I kept it straight. This one had the reducing joint to go on to the six-inch jarrah pipe. The sledge was now rolled on to its side and the heavy pipe eased out into the mud and then down a bit for the reducing joint to fit in.

I now began pulling the sledge back, halfway up my gumboots in mud. The job became more difficult as we got further up in the slippery rockface, about halfway up. It took a whole hour to get each pipe up and fitted into place. The two men who had thought they had seen everything and nothing more was possible to startle them, suddenly gave a frantic yell —

Dudley Badham Snr was the first Patron of the Surf Club, manager and sponsor. Here he is (at far left) at the first surf carnival at Browns Bay. He had donated the flag and wooden reel to the club.

The Karekare Surf Life Saving Club's Roll of Honour, which is mounted on The Watchman, includes Dudley and John Badham.

'My God!' I had decided the quickest way to get the sledge back down the 60° face was to stand on it and let it go, giving the fork a kick with my foot as we went to keep it straight. At the bottom I swung it round ready for the next pipe and looked up to see them staring at me as if I had just dropped from the moon.

That night they had nightmares and my mother told me next morning she had heard them calling out in their sleep, thinking they had seen me fall off and roll to the bottom. We all had a good laugh at breakfast and they thought it was no joke as they knew they would have to watch the performance six or seven times a day for several days yet. I got quite good at it by then.

As we were now on the steep part the work became more difficult and it was necessary to rig up a block and endless chain to hold the heavy pipe. I fixed this to another big ti-tree and the pipe was then secured before being rolled out of the box. My father, Dudley and myself had to work with one hand now and hold on to a rope with the other to prevent falling down the steep face.

With the pipe out of the box I carefully worked the box to one side so we could lower the pipe held with the block and chain into position. You can now see why it took a whole hour to get each pipe up into place. With that accomplished I turned the sledge round and stood in it, racing away to the bottom like an express train.

On the afternoon of the fourth day the manager of the Hulm Pipe Co. arrived to see what was going on. Used to his men laying 170-a-day on flat ground he thought they must be enjoying themselves fishing or looking for mermaids. The shock his two men got when they first saw where the pipes had to go was multiplied several times when he saw what we were doing.

Two days later the last pipe was in place and the two men returned to Auckland leaving my father, Dudley and myself to finish off. This consisted of hanging on by the skins of our teeth again while making four holes in the rock by each pipe to get two steel bolts, bent like an inverted 'n', round each end of the pipe and then cemented in to the rock to prevent it from swaying with the terrific pressure of water, which 80 pounds to the square inch at the bottom of the 180 foot drop.

After several more days of toil we at last finished the job and could put the water back in and have the electric light.

1938

The year 1938 was to be an eventful year in several ways. First, my cousin Woee Farley at Whatipu was to disappear on Thursday 31 March. The following morning I was working up the Skids Gulley with Mr Jim Ruddell and Mr Tom Scott getting ti-tree firewood out, when I heard the frantic blowing of a whistle. This for years had always been a signal that something was wrong, so I said to the men that I would have to go and see what the trouble was.

I should now say that the people at the house had all gone to town for the day except my mother, me and Erin Lockie, who was working for us at the time. When I got to the road near the old engine shed I found her nearly blowing her front teeth out. She jumbled one word into another. I finally made out that Uncle Wally Farley had rung through from Whatipu to say that Woee was missing and his fishing line had been found tangled round the wharf steps. On the wharf was his fishing bag, with spare lines and hooks. He must have gone down sometime the previous night. The first they knew of it was when his sister June noticed that the cows had not been brought up and his bed had not been slept in.

As I hurried back with Erin she said the family wanted me to go and have a look down the beach, which I did, though I didn't think it was much good.

After I came back from the beach my mother asked me what I thought. I said I was puzzled as I thought Woee was far too familiar with it all to be caught off guard in any way. One thing I do know and that is the sea very seldom gives up any bodies if anyone drowned in the vicinity of the Manukau Heads. Many have been drowned there over the years and very few bodies ever recovered. The wharf steps and fishing bag on the wharf did not prove that he fell in the water.

I did not say anything to my mother or anyone about a strange thing that happened to me on the night of the 31st. Some time during the night I woke

This postcard memento was given and sold to guests of the boarding house.

and it was like someone was shaking me to warn me that something was wrong. I have thought a lot about it over the years and the fact that Woee and I worked together on the farm from the summer of 1930 till May 1932 when he went to Whatipu no doubt had some bearing on my feeling.

My brother Dudley, who was working in town, came home for the weekend and he and I walked round to Whatipu the following morning to see the family. We went straight to the wharf and had a look round, though I knew it was no good. After a discussion, we made straight for the house and found them all sitting on the verandah, looking very puzzled. Wally Farley said to the girls to give us some lunch; after finishing that and talking it over there was nothing more that could be done except watch the beach. On the ninth day we left for home. On Saturday 9 April I left on my own for Whatipu as I had planned to buy Kathleen's horse, Peter, and knew I would meet some of them looking from that end. I met her on the horse at Pararaha and we walked back to Whatipu without any sign. Not a trace of him was ever found and it is just as much a mystery today, after all these years.

After a cup of tea Kathleen said goodbye to her horse and I swung into the saddle and made for home at a gallop as the tide was coming in and I had to get him over the Karekare Point. Arriving at the Point I dismounted to climb on the rocks behind me. He knew it all and followed close behind, carefully stepping over the slippery sleepers where the engine used to run, 20 years earlier. Back at the house I put Peter in the calf paddock where he would be easy to catch if I wanted him in a hurry for my stock work.

I was now starting to work the farm up as an efficient part of the organisation and had for some time thought of introducing a breed of run cattle. My choice was the Polled Hereford, a breed without horns. The first stage of getting them on to the farm was when I burnt the area of the Point in late February 1937.

The second stage was to build a good set of cattle yards. I chose the spot just at the back of the old engine shed and on the high bank of the creek. This made an ideal spot to drive them in from all directions. With a Taranaki-gate style the fence could be run out to the side of a small hill where they were trapped before they knew it. If being driven this way from the Skids Gully they came along the same track that the engine used to haul the bolsters of timber 20 years earlier. If being driven from the top of the paddocks or Dunholm Gully the wing fence could be reversed and run the other way. The posts were puriri and were seven feet out of the ground, while the rails were long straight split puriri. These yards took a while to construct and with the busy season of Christmas and then Easter, nothing could be done then except for a little work by hired help.

With Easter over and the winter of 1938 coming in I carried on getting ti-tree cut and clearing and fencing. There was a sale at Tuakau advertised for 10 October, so my father and I left to attend in the 1929 seven-seater Studebaker. My father bought two bulls, one two-year-old and a three-year-old. I bought one two-year-old branded 171. They were all fine looking cattle, coming off 5000 acres at Glen Murray.

We arranged for the animals to be sent by rail to Glen Eden the next day and we got home in time for milking. A drover, Mr Bob Gordon of Huia, was going to drive them from Glen Eden. On Wednesday 11 October my father and I were going to town and I was to drive a 1926 Hudson truck home for the farm.

When we got to Glen Eden they were just going to let our animals out of the cattle truck so I rushed over to help as they opened the door. I did not realise that they had not waited for their heads to face the door before opening it. The result was one came out and the other two were facing the wrong way. I was between a railway wagon and a high bank and this one, which was the three year old, could not see the other two, which were still in the truck, and came straight for me. I could not get into the wagon and the bank was too high, so when he nearly got to me with his head down I threw myself on to his shoulder. This spun me round and I fell on the loose metal of the station yard, breaking my cheekbone and at the same time clipping my front tooth. The bull just carried on and ended up in the Glen Eden Reserve, while I picked myself up and my father rushed over and took me into the chemist shop. I was a bit shaken up and when they saw what had happened to my tooth, instead of driving the truck home I had to go to the dentist and get it fixed up. The dentist, Mr Tibbs, was a chap who used to come out to Karekare and he had to ask a lady who was in the chair if she could come back the next day as I had met with an accident. He made an excellent job of it having to put it on a brace with a gold base at the back. It lasted for 30 years and was still sound when I had my last few top teeth out so it had to come also.

Before leaving Glen Eden for town with me, my father and Bob Gordon had decided to leave the bulls where they were and for Bob to go through to Karekare and get some of the dry cows to bring back and put with them for the drive out. When my father and I got home, Bob Gordon was there and he spent the night, leaving the next morning with half-a-dozen cows. I can only remember the name of one of them, a brown-and-white called Trixie, who I thought would be a good leader for the trip home.

My mother was worried about me but I said I was okay and did the milking as usual. The bulls arrived on Friday; Bob Gordon had to get another drover to help him bring them through. Trixie, who knew she was nearly home, set the pace coming down the Cutting.

I saw them coming along the flat as I was on the lookout. I rushed to open the gate into the right paddock by the Norfolk pines. As I have said before, the pines were planted at the grave of the little girl who drowned in the creek, about 1880. The next morning Bob Gordon and I put two of the bulls, my one and the big three-year old, up on Karekare Point, leaving Mangatea Forester with the milking cows in the valley. With the summer of 1938 coming on we thought it best to only have the one round the house.

Mangatea used to wait outside the yard while the milking was done, keeping the sightseers and campers away from coming up to get milk. The shop was the place for that so he was doing me a good turn. The summer of 1938 was a busy one and although he kept them away from the milking yard, he was powerless to prevent the occasional Kamikaze act in the surf that left never a dull moment, particularly if it occurred in the middle of dinner.

1939

I had been fortunate to have the opportunity to go on a hunting trip south of Rotorua in the early part of 1939 and I returned refreshed and ready to get back to the farm. The first thing I did the morning after I arrived back was round up the stock in the valley and then go to the Point to look at the Hereford bulls and some steers with dry cows that I had put there.

Before long it was Easter and a busy time again for a few days and then the quieter time of the winter. There were the dances on a Saturday night, sometimes in the Karekare Hall, then at the Blow Hole and the Piha Hall alternately. This gave us a chance to meet our neighbours, have a yarn and find out if there had been any development, or if anyone had gone bush and got caught in a possum trap. In this way the winter passed along and then the spring came.

The next event was momentous; there had been dark clouds gathering over Europe for quite a while and I will never forget the evening of Sunday 3 September 1939. We were all sitting round the open fire in the little sitting room that Mr Charlie Hyde had built for my grandmother after finishing the cottage on The Watchman in 1928.

There was no TV then and we suddenly heard on the radio the voice of Mr Neville Chamberlain, the Prime Minister of Great Britain, saying the time-limit for Hitler to withdraw his troops from Poland had passed. So a state of war now existed between Britain and France and Germany.

None of us knew then just how long it would last, but I felt we were in for a long hard struggle. I was right; the war lasted from 3 September 1939 till 16 August 1945.

At home the first thing to jolt the powers that be in New Zealand out of their apathy that was a product of the geographical distance from Europe, was when the *Niagara*, which had gold in her cargo, struck a mine off the Hen and Chicken Islands and sunk in 485 feet of water. All but two of the gold bars were recovered after the war was over.

Wally Badham, 1939.

After the war, I read a book written by the captain of the German raider *Orion*, which laid the mines in the Hauraki Gulf. The captain said that while crossing the Indian Ocean to come here his men were greatly amused by our radio stations broadcasting weather reports every hour. Our radio stations blurted out the sinking of the *Niagara*, which was also picked up by the raiders as they steamed up round the Kermadec Islands.

All we had that could go that far out to sea to look for the culprit was one of Tasman Airways flying boats, the *Aotearoa*, which was promptly sent out. It was fitted up for carrying paying passengers and not adaptable for dropping any kind of bombs. The aircraft was seen by the raiders, who were astounded to see a plane so far from land, but stranger still the crew of the aircraft never saw them, so the war steamed merrily on.

Advertising for Winchelsea and Whatipu houses, which appeared in *The Weekly News*, 14 October 1940.

1942

My name had been down for the Air Force for a while. At that time Japan joined Germany and Italy, with the attack on Pearl Harbour on 7 December 1941 and drove south alarmingly quickly. By February 1942 Singapore had gone and everything north of Australia was in Japanese hands.

At a World War II lookout camp on Ridge Road, Anawhata. Dudley Badham Snr, Wally's father, third from right.

I was rushed into a Special Army Unit and did a Commando course at Narrowneck after being sent into the bush at Anawhata with Mr John Chisholm of Henderson, Mr Neville Ussher and my father. We had secret instructions and we worked from a base camp up the Ridge Road just below the property known as Simla. We tramped all through the Waitakere Ranges and round behind Whenuapai and Hobsonville air bases. The other three remained in the bush camp up the Ridge Road while I was at Narrowneck on the Commando course. After rejoining them I was able to go with them on their trips. One morning before daylight we were all woken up by a terrific bang. Was it a bomb from an enemy plane? Was it a shell from an enemy submarine or just a domestic argument? We could only wonder and keep our rifles ready and watch for any civilians fleeing into the bush. The next day we got instructions to leave our base camp and reconnoitre round the back of Hobsonville and Whenuapai air bases. Although it was hush-hush we found out what the big bang had been. A United States Air Force B-17 Flying Fortress had crashed while taking off from Whenuapai.

Complete secrecy surrounded the mission and after inspecting the big hole in the ground I was sure it was caused by engine failure in the take-off. With a full load of bombs on board the aircraft exploded on impact with the ground, hence the big bang that we heard at our bush camp.

After making a close study of both aerodromes from the hills we continued on to Brighams Creek, sleeping in an old wagon in a shed. We had John Chisholm's horse as a packhorse and I was in charge of it.

Edward, Dudley, Wallace, John and Zoe Badham, 1942.

After a somewhat sleepless night we continued on to Waimauku, where we had lunch and a spell before going on to Muriwai. The last time I had seen Muriwai was from the air in ZK-AAK in September 1933, when I made a flight down the coast and came low over the house at Karekare and shook them all up before doing the same at Whatipu.

After leaving Waimauku we continued on to Muriwai, arriving mid-afternoon. After a short spell we carried on to Bethells at Te Henga. I was leading the horse all the time, which was carrying our packs and was usually out in front.

The afternoon sun was sinking and we still had some distance to go when we came to a fence. There seemed no way of getting the horse through. We all started looking round and I hitched the bridle to the fence as I set off to look for a gate. After a while I had just about given up when I came across a Taranaki gate and the predicament was over.

John Chisholm was hell-bent on finding an old maimai that someone had told him about and where he wanted to spend the night. While he was looking for it and as it was starting to get dark, my sharp ears picked up the sound of a stationary engine which I knew would be at Bethells.

I pushed on with the horse on my own and came out of the valley on to the beach, crossed the creek and made for the sound, which was getting louder. I came round a corner and suddenly saw all the lights of Bethells'; both the horse and I gave a sigh of relief. John Chisholm could not find his old maimai and as it was getting darker he, my father and Neville Ussher came round the corner to find me explaining things to the Bethells. They had been down fishing that afternoon and gave us a good dinner and comfortable bed for the night.

The next morning, before going on to our base camp at Anawhata, we went to have a look at the lake known as Bethells Lake. After a close look at the lake that Pa Bethell often said he would swap any time for the Karekare Waterfall, we said thanks to the Bethells and set off for Anawhata via Simla.

Out in front with the horse it was another day's tramp in rough country. We reached Simla late in the afternoon. Before the Waitakere Dam was built, a road continued from the top of Mountain Road down to the Waitakere Stream and up the other side to Simla. The property was owned by Mr Bill Notting, who had named the property after Simla in India, where his father, an officer in the Indian Army, was stationed.

Wally's wife, Irene Isabel Badham (née Edwards) and their year-old son, Warwick, at Piha.

Before 1950 there was a farm gate at the head of the Karekare Valley, which needed to be opened (and of course closed) on leaving. The posts were visible at the side of the road until the 1970s.

Epilogue
Lisa Fallow

I first met Wally when I became interested in the family history, around 1991, and wanted to find out more information. Everyone said to talk to Wally and, because he only lived a small distance away, I made arrangements to go and see him.

Wally lived in a small unit in Alexander Street in Howick, Auckland. He had always been eccentric, which I think is a nice way to put it! His house was very dirty and smelly.

The first trial in visiting Wally at home was trying to get in the door. He always had budgies flying around in the house and only put them in the cage at night, when he moved them into his bedroom with him. I remember Mum inviting him over for Christmas one day when I was little and he couldn't leave his budgies behind, so they had to come too. These budgies were always called 'Buddy', even when he had two or three at a time. When I had to clean up the unit after he was in the home, I had to prise the beautiful antique embroideries off the walls because they were all stuck to the wallpaper with years' worth of bird poo.

Wally also had cats, which he did not let in the house (of course because of the budgies). These he fed on the doorstep. Each year they would have kittens, which Wally would drown in the bathtub. I tried to get him to let me get the cats spayed and neutered, but he said that it took their hunting instinct away from them and he wouldn't let me. I did save one stripy, grey kitten that we called Troi; she turned out to be an exceptionally fine pet.

Wally was a mine of information about the family. He lived for the days back at Karekare and this was all he could ever talk about. After some time he showed me the book he had written when his niece Raewyn suggested he should write down all he knew. He was very proud of this book; only after many visits did I manage to get him to agree to me making a photocopy of it so I could type it out for him. He would only let the book go for one day, so I had to get it all copied in one go.

Now, typing up someone else's book is not hard, but Wally had the worst handwriting I had ever seen and I had to teach myself how to read it. I would highlight all the words I didn't know and take it round to Wally for him to tell me what was what. I got so good at reading it that the only words I couldn't make out, Wally had no idea about either.

This took a long time and many, many visits to Wally's house, over which time I think we got to know each other pretty well. Wally came to see that I had a genuine interest in what he knew and could tell me. He also started bringing out 'little treasures' that he had inherited from his mother Zoe when she died. Each time I went over there would be more things for me to see and more stories for him to tell. It got to the stage where I had heard them all so many times I could start to correct him about things, but never dates. Wally was fantastic with dates.

In 1995 I went over to San Diego for six months, during which time Wally had a fall while walking to Howick. He was taken away in an ambulance and the Social Welfare Department got him on the books as needing some help, which we all knew, but he was set against it.

Wally never let anyone into the back of his house; when Social Welfare came to see what help he would need in his home they discovered an entire room, at the back of the house, filled to the roof with empty cat tins. The RSA supplied a dumper to put them in. He also got four hours worth of housekeeping each week but he never let the lady anywhere but the lounge and kitchen, even though she protested about it.

I kept visiting Wally and bringing him food to eat on the weekends, when Meals on Wheels didn't come. He would sometimes pop over to the bakery at the back of his house to get a pie and to have a chat with them. Every birthday he would order a sponge cake with cream from them to eat, by himself at home, after taking a photo of it.

Eventually Wally started getting worse and worse. He would call me in the morning to say he had fallen over in the night and could not get up. I would have to go round there to pick him up and see if he was okay. I had talked to him about going into a home but he was adamant that he wanted to stay at home; at that stage that was still his decision to make.

His friends Pat and Tony came around one day to find that he had fallen down and hurt himself. They called the ambulance to get him to hospital. They also rang me and I went off with him. The doctor sent him home with me because the hospital was full and I said I would look after him. But Wally couldn't feed himself, let alone get out of bed to go to the toilet and eventually I had to get the hospital to take him in. Once he was in there and having antibiotics and lots of attention he was fine. After a short while they discharged him to go home by himself.

Every day I would ring him in the morning to see if he answered and if not I would go around to help him up. I tried Social Welfare and they were no good, so in desperation I rang the Baptist Home where his cleaning lady came from and talked to their social workers. They were fabulous and even though he was not one of their clients and they were full at their home, they arranged to meet me at Wally's one day. I got there about two minutes before they did to find Wally on the floor of his bedroom again. He had wet clothes on as he had tried but failed to get up to go to the toilet in the night. The visitors took one look at him and jumped into action. They managed to find a rest home that would take him and off Wally went to the Edgewater Nursing Home.

I was very upset but relieved at the same time. Wally was very sick with pneumonia when he was first in the home, but with all the attention and good food lavished on him, not to mention the company, he bounced back. Wally still thought that this was going to be a temporary stay in hospital, but it was soon evident even to him that he was not capable of staying at home by himself. He had many little falls and got the odd bruise. He loved the nurses and gave them a hard time. He also liked being around people who had never heard his jokes before. I was looking after his budgie in the meantime. Once I had permission from the matron to bring the budgie in for Wally, which she agreed to as long as I cleaned the cage.

He stayed in this home and he became one of the regulars. He was treated well there, but he always had some complaint when I went to see him: 'They put too much food on my plate.' 'They make me have a shower too often.' 'They changed the seating plan for dinner.' 'They keep opening my window in my room when I'm not there.'

After he had been there a month we decided it was time to let his rented unit go. I got the lovely job of cleaning out his house. To say Wally was a hoarder is an understatement. There were piles of rubbish everywhere, but amongst the rubbish were treasures, so each stack of old newspapers or electricity bills for the entire time Wally had been there had to be sorted through. I also found the remains of all his old budgies, which he had ritually cremated on the gas heater after taking a photo of them lying on a special red pillow.

Wally was happy in the home, even though he had the odd case of pneumonia and they had to keep forcing him to drink anything; he said, 'I don't like to drink because then you just have to get up to get rid of it later.' He had a love-hate relationship with the Matron because she made him do horrible things like sit up in the lounge when he had pneumonia so that his lungs wouldn't fill up with water, and she was the one who changed the seating arrangements every three months so that you were sitting with new people. She also made him go for the odd drive in the van when she took people out, instead of staying in his room for 22 hours a day.

He loved his room and always kept the radio on so that Buddy would have something to listen to. He also had a supply of biscuits, which I brought in for him each week. I could always tell how he was feeling by how the biscuit supply was.

One day I got a phone call from the Matron to say that Wally had fallen down some steps and cut his head badly. He had been unconscious for quite a while and had been taken to hospital. He had also broken his hip and would need an operation to fix it.

He had to be in traction for a couple of days before they could operate because he had a bit of pneumonia and they didn't want to operate on him in that condition. Wally was very out of it and terribly confused the entire time he was in hospital. I went to visit him every day and he was always so pleased to see me. Apparently he would be calling out for me all the time. The doctors thought there might have been something wrong mentally with him, but it was just that he was so confused with all the different staff and surroundings. His world had become very small and this was too much for him. The Matron was a lifesaver; she said she would take him back to the home even though he should still be in hospital.

Wally was so pleased to be back at the home. He was hugging and kissing all the nurses, although he was still a bit confused as he was moved in to a different room because his old room was too narrow for the nurses to get the wheelchair in easily and manoeuvre him. He thought he was living at the Matron's house, in her front room. Wally insisted that the accident had happened when he was out riding a white horse to get the cows in and he fell off.

He never really recovered from this fall. His mobility was severely limited and he could not really walk without help. This didn't stop him from trying though and he had a couple of falls when he tried to walk by himself. In the end the staff loosely tied his dressing gown cord around him and the chair and put the knot behind the chair where he couldn't see it. It didn't constrict him at all but it meant he could not get up without them.

It was at this time that he stopped eating. When he did start again he would eat only sweet things! He complained to me one time, 'I don't want anything in my mouth if it's not sweet. They tried to give me something the other day and it was not sweet enough.' This 'thing' turned out to be a scone with jam on it.

It was obvious at this stage that Wally was not going to live for much longer. His body was shutting down, his kidneys were not working and he had pneumonia. The doctor wanted him to go in to hospital but I had promised Wally that he would never have to go back there after the last time. The matron agreed with me and said unless something really serious happened she was happy for him to finish his days there.

As previously mentioned, Wally often alluded to his youth as being the best time of his life; again we might speculate that he did not enjoy or experience the rest of his life as joyfully as he did those early years. Wally went out to Karekare one last time with Bob Harvey. He came back tired, but happy and at peace. Over the next few months he seemed to close down and slip away. His life came to a gentle end.

Photo acknowledgements

The publisher is grateful to the following institutions that have granted permission to reproduce the following photographs, and in particular to Waitakere Library and Information Services for assistance with identification and scanning. Unless noted, all other images are courtesy the Badham family and Bob Harvey.

References are to page numbers; t = top, m= middle, b = bottom, l = left, r = right; image library reference numbers are in brackets

Special Collections, Auckland City Libraries
23l (4-1463)

Alexander Turnbull Library
51r (APG-0354-1/2-G), 52 (APG-0355-1/2-G), 55 (APG-0689-1/2-G), 56r (APG-0349-1/2-G), 57br (APG-0672-1/2-G), 58l (APG-0382-1/2-G), 59br (APG-0685-1/2-G), 66 (APG-0834-1/2-G), 82r (APG-0662-1/2-G), 156 (G-7146-1/2, Radcliffe Collection)

Auckland War Memorial Museum
32t (A283/DU436), 90t (C30283)

Waitakere Library and Information Services
12 (Waitakere Library and Information Services Newspaper Collection), 20t (Waitakere Library and Information Services Print Collection), 56l (J.T. Diamond Collection (05C) 01078.3), 90 (J.T. Diamond Collection (08B) 1075.G), 190 (Waitakere Library and Information Services Newspaper Collection)

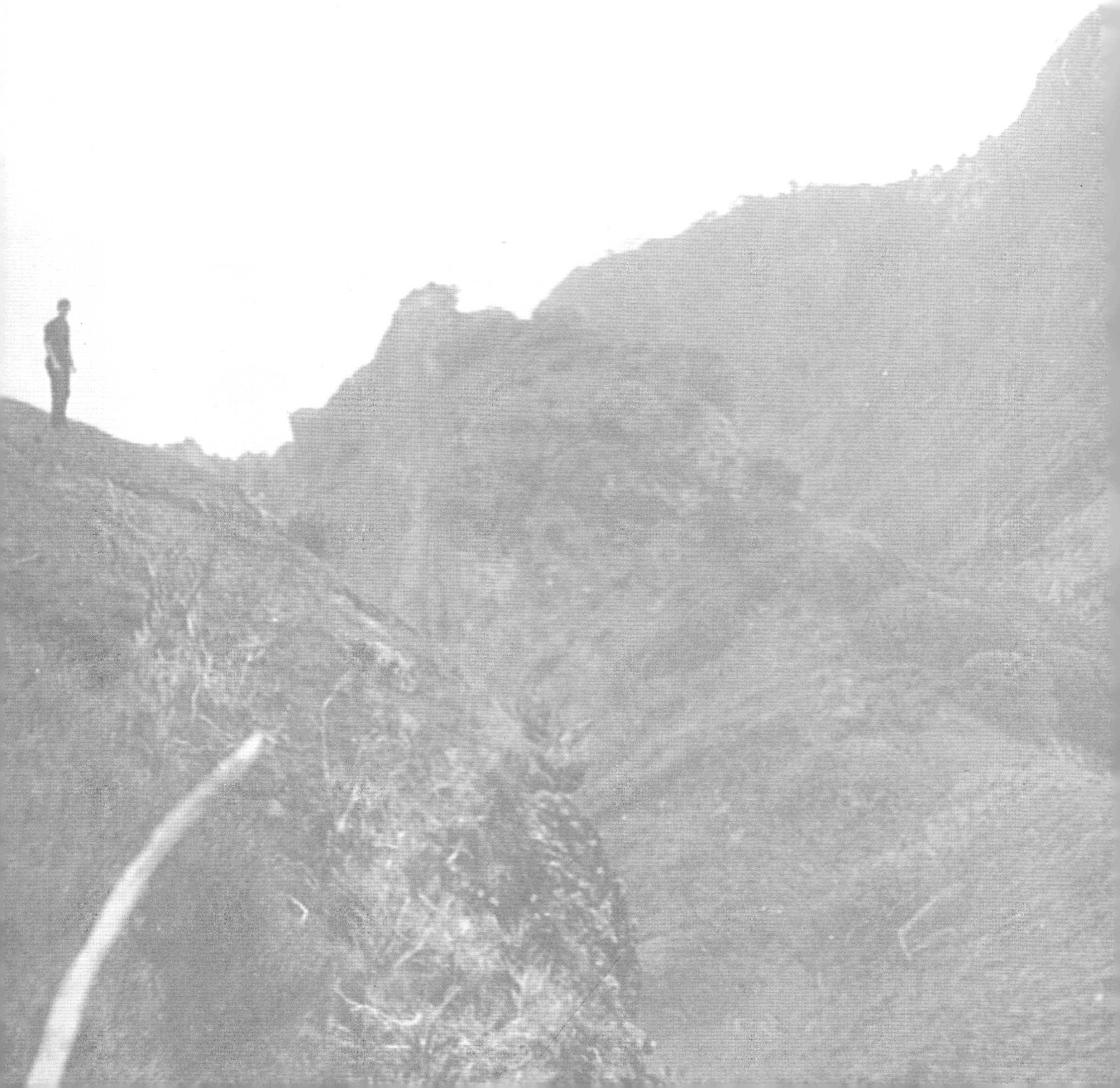